AHSAHTA PRESS | BOISE IDAHO

THE NEW SERIES | #90

HOW THE UNIVERSE IS MADE

POEMS NEW & SELECTED

1985–2019

STEPHANIE STRICKLAND

Ahsahta Press, Boise State University, Boise, Idaho 83725-1580
Cover design by Quemadura
Book design by Janet Holmes
ahsahtapress.org
Copyright © 2019 by Stephanie Strickland

LIBRARY OF CONGRESS CATALOGING-IN-PUBLICATION DATA

Names: Strickland, Stephanie, author.
Title: How the universe is made : poems new & selected, 1985–2019 / Stephanie
    Strickland.
Description: Boise, Idaho : Ahsahta Press, [2019] | Series: The new series ;
    #90
Identifiers: LCCN 2018038002| ISBN 9781934103876 (pbk. : alk. paper) | ISBN
    193410387X (pbk. : alk. paper)
Classification: LCC PS3569.T69543 A6 2019 | DDC 811/.54—dc23
LC record available at https://lccn.loc.gov/2018038002

ABOUT THE COVER

Micronesian stick charts show wave patterns and currents. The shells represent atolls and islands. Ancient mariners navigated thousands of miles, without compasses, astrolabes, or any mechanical device, using only their bodies and their highly individualized, often memorized, charts.

LINEAGE-LINKAGE-HOMAGE

Lorine Niedecker

Tim Lilburn

Kitasono Katue

SIMONE WEIL

Christina McPhee

Muriel Rukeyser
Willard Gibbs

Xu Bing
Tianshu (Book from the Sky)

Bertolt Brecht
Die Liebenden

Wallace Stevens

LAKE ST. CLAIR

Thomas Hardy
The Mellstock Quire

Mez
The data][h!][bleeding
t.ex][e]ts

Joan Retallack
The Poethical Wager

Laura Riding *The Telling*

Audre Lorde *Sister Outsider*

Susan Howe
The Birth-Mark

Nathaniel Mackey

Gerard Manley Hopkins

Mother   Goose

SELECTED POEMS

GIVE THE BODY BACK

SEEING A MEDUSA

Only that tinge of crimson-pink
like cyclamen flashing
drew me down, made me see you

in the heave of the wake, all
pale-jelly innard
on your side, resisting nothing

in the wash of green glass, clear gray, the waves
calm today, steady, as you slap
up and down in their hands— a nest

of tentacles rolling with the foam,
then hanging, white with poison. You collapse
an inbreath of water, shudder. Glide.

Gone, before I grew faint
leaning over the boat; gone,
before I even knew

it was you—alive! Not knowing. Reliving
the blow, remembering: you, torn out, despised
and flung dripping to the waves.

MOTHER: DRESSED UP

A veil's tiny
black diamonds touch
your lashes, your cheeks.

Perfume ringing
from your wrist, you lean
sideways

on the stair;
your brim, your lips just
brush me.

Faraway,
mild, your eyes
lift to him:

I am stunned
by your body, trying
to hide

its eagerness
to pull away
from mine.

MY MOTHER'S BODY

Moved through
like a dune, become the sweep
of a palm through sand, my mother's body
became like sand, breached, a memory
of outline. Her lungs
fill with water, a hull overturned, sails
filling with water, toss, stiffen
in the sunlight. Again
submerge.
Breath at long intervals. Needle-flow
of bubbles in the respirator.
Pure oxygen
forced through her mouth, drying
her lips. "Look,
I've brought gloss. Pomade. I know—
you don't want
smell. No, this has no scent,
no color."
Only her eyebrows.
"Don't wash off my eyebrows,"
she says. They are like wings
of soft brown powder that go nowhere, stopped
at the arch in flight.
This room
crowds her so, even
its light. I push back the flowers.
She loves my father.
She opens
her arms as if the tubes and bandages and wires
were Titania's cape in the moonlight.
"Tell me about writing . . . ."
But
I could not tell her.

LOVE THAT GIVES US OURSELVES: MURIEL RUKEYSER

She said disowning
is the only treason. She said we pretend
coldness, or pretend
we are used to the world.
She said
all I touch has failed,
and the beginning was real.
She said, by imagining
the child can cope with loss,
be at home.
It is a work of images, difficult
and bare. Very slow. Like falling in love,
desire shadows its fulfillment.
She said
now I speak only words I can believe,
no sly resonant pity.
Her short questions, the gravel
of her answers comes back to me again
and again, in waves:
turn with your whole life choosing.
Everything here is real, she said,
and of our joy. Her mother
· didn't answer. Even past death
language incomplete
between them. Intense
desire scorches its fulfillment.

SWEAT

If I laugh louder now, unfrightened,
dream dreams to their conclusion,
the face of my mother as a young woman
close to my face, both of us, two of us
wrestling closer and closer on a bed,

if I don't stop the dream, if I don't let
the seizures wake me completely
—these are people I know, whose faces
I know, my husband, dreamed,
who sleeps at my breast, restless,

if I am less afraid
of what I lose—of the connection
I am to all I lose; if I care less
that I'm cruel, marked
by my father's grit, his invitation;

if I dream of blood, of Hathor's rage
appeased by a deception, the field soaked
with red beer, of Isis as a falcon
ravishing the corpse, and laugh aloud
touching men and women; if I tire of this

and sleep, and if my mother,
a young woman, grips me so tight
with her arms and legs that I am filled
with torment, with a kind of light
which makes me speak

in the dream, say *I love you so*;
later sweat with this blessing,
think, where are you now?
Have you come to me now?
It is not too late.

CONSORT

And what did that make her?
Forcing him to do it. She didn't like
insistence, only because she could never pace

or gauge it—faster: his panic burning off, buried
in her pores like mist. No distance; skin,
whose it was, whose limb even, unclear.

She didn't like binding him,
full of being bound. She liked amnesia:
each day to discover another

sun, sinking on both, for both the same,
almost; more gold on his face
and fish-hook grin, more solar pressure on her hip

when she limped. She liked
no cog, no evident intent, no emotion at all—
except surprise: the cooled orange of carrots torn

into strange air, circles of greenlight
feathering, enfolding them, lifted away:
holes in the ground

redug toward water, and deeper, toward garnet needles
bursting their matrix, spike after spike
like Viking boats,

like stars
in an Arctic night. And darker still, wider,
still exactly what she was.

THE OLD WOMAN SAID

"You think I'm too old
to know what it is?
I know it better than my life.
Don't tell your grandmother how
to suck eggs, Miss. Don't murmur me
desire—a stigma, a block
and not natural," she said, "not
natural enough,
but what they don't teach it,
throw it in your eyes. Look here
child, it's no mean trick
staying alive
in those shells of desire.
Look at your mother's
mission: bleed to feel. 'If
she so *chooses*.'
They put that in, but the truth
of it is, no one refuses,
no one and nothing not part
of the terror
driving that bargain: I make,
you eat— Child, there's teeth
in every mouth that waters. You've got
to watch out
for the din of the women, moaning
'Take care, only one thing they want,'
that you don't lose your nerve.
The lie about love
is that it isn't
here. You can feel desire.
Desire is a rouge dress
glowing in the dark. Or it doesn't
glow—but it never comes off:

an oil to conform,
or a chain to control,
the body. The body, child,
is a soul, injured at birth
by people's talk.
It's a shock how harsh, ugly
sometimes, the acts of love
can look. And child, they're not,
ever, what you expect
or want,
because they leave nothing
to language, no more than a drop
shining on a sieve. You
will know them:
they give the body back."

AT SEA

It will float now she thinks;
she has hollowed it
enough. Numbness spreads in
her shoulder, her swollen wrist,
arms lying on the rocker.
Oil lamp in the rafters.
Feet bare on the dirt floor.
She does not remember,
anymore, what is undone—only
the boat, blued with indigo,
brilliant. Single lamp
in the rafters. Blue with indigo
her fingers. He is brilliant, pine
silver, perfect husband, sea-
husband, ready strength, swirling
peace . . . . Dozing, starts up
to shake her rattle; flames
tatter above her in the open hut.
On the swept floor, pillows
with lace, conch shells, roses.
In a night filled with sounds,
the sound of her fan, falling
on her lap. Imperceptibly
rocking, all alone, guarding
the bed. Perfect husband,
sea-husband, who, if he comes,
comes and goes with a roar mild
as mist, in the grizzled
light, mild as any morning
mist, in the first light,
when she finally sleeps,
when the rocker is stopped.

LIVING ON AIR

1

Exact and tyrannical
intelligence in women: in their bodies. Not ventriloquy,
acumen: the splintered eye refusing
a caduceus, a tree-of-life, or any surface wholeness
to swirl beakers of light. Bodies of women
constructing two solutions from the same vinegared
mother, whose uncleaving polarizes light: black,
or bright, a light that can't pass till it's twisted.
Discovered in acid
crystals of new wine by an indifferent eye. Hard
and indifferent. Like the body of a woman
defenseless with what it knows, feeling this happen
too many times. My sinister hand
unlike the right one, now; and my greenhouse
not a solarium. The cockatoo has gone
and in its place a raven crazed
by lighted space.

2

Unlike myself, in the secret divisions
which feel like truth because they are sealed
off, I invite
the man with gloves to come closer.
His black cloth hood with slits as familiar to me
as the rocking boat he steps out of: a ferryman
of bodies, a liminal human who complies
in all silence;
unlike the body of any woman,
unlike the voice of the woman who tells me, tear it out,

that tree of live wire crusting with seed pearls
rooted in your blood. He climbs this tree
of eels, swings his axe
with both hands. Footgear, posture, oarlock: all one
gesture, repeating its meaning, condemned
to repeat it. After all, I am alone here,

3

in the fall of the year. In my greenhouse. The ceiling
sways, glittering with shockwaves.
Pouches of splinter hang. Nubbles of crystal
fill the small craters crushed against
the mesh skeleton. Citrin
and olive patterns of light harlequin
my body, as if this were a dome of stained glass overhead
and its broken places, mazes of solder. The whole sky
is tender with smoke. Muted rose
suffuses the November dusk,
rising from the city like a philtre, or a promise,
and not what it is, lost darkness.

4

The doors that lead out, the French doors, are dismantled,
stored in the cellar on a broken workbench.
There's damp in the dirt floor. Some of the pumpkins
do not rot
as soon as the others; some wither: dried fibers
draw their teeth inward, bit by bit, the grin
becoming a wince.

Like the body of a woman, betrayed. Sheets of newsprint
swirl on the ground, falter in the doorway
on a skewer of wind; swept forward,
a puppet of rubbish, litter, in whose eyes I read again:
Strange chemical reactions in the old beams set
St. Luke's afire. They were not strange.
Don't call them strange, you, who depart,
and never regain,
bodies of women, living on air, all of them, on air;
as you, on air.

THE RED VIRGIN: A POEM OF SIMONE WEIL

As for the Red Virgin,
we shall leave it to her to make bombs for the coming grand
social upheaval . . .

we shall send the Red Virgin
as far away as possible so that we shall never
hear of her again.

C. BOUGLÉ, ACTING DIRECTOR, ÉCOLE NORMALE SUPÉRIEURE
DIRECTOR OF CAREER PLACEMENT

ABSENT FROM DANCES, 1925

Black, Byzantine eyes
seize us like falcons.
We are defended, a bit,

by the wire-rims;
by lips, unreasonably
full. Awkward hips, long

tent skirts. Stuffing an inkpot
down the pocket
of her beige one—the stains,

huge, black suns
spreading on
the skirtfront, Simone!

at sixteen
you should have been more lady-
like, less mood, less

burning.
At fourteen,
I thought of dying.

My brother, his exceptional
gifts, brought
my own

inferiority
home to me. I did not mind
the lack of visible

successes . . . what did
grieve me . . . being excluded— Truth
reserved for genius.

AGENT

How do you say her?

          Simone. Say Simone.

But she signs
her letters, *Your affectionate
son, Simon*—

     she's divided,
     always going half-way,
     a double agent.

How do you say Weil?

     Not *Vile,* not the German,
     although I would be pleased
     to call her *Miss Because,*

     but as the family said it,
     Vyay, Vey, an oversound
     of woe, of one

     who waits, keeps vigil.
     To us, a *way* away,
     unavailing.

1. *Send me. I'll organize a Front Line Corps*
   of Nurses. Men, who would otherwise die from shock
   and loss of blood, will live. Send me.

   Rejected.

2. *Since Nazis are inflamed by prestige, by the mystique*
   of the SS, the persistence of services offered
   at great risk, from great love, in the center
   of our battles, will serve as a symbol, a rallying
   image. I will train the women. Send me.

   Rejected.

3. Morale *is* decisive. Though not better armed,
   the Germans sweep Belgium, leave Paris exposed.
   The French call in old men, Weygand
   as commander. *I want to be*
   in Weygand's shoes, Simone tells her friend.

   She—a Pacifist?

4. June 13, 1940. Overnight on the wall,
   PARIS—OPEN CITY—WILL NOT BE DEFENDED.
   Mme. Weil out strolling with her husband
   and Simone sees the sign, makes them run
   to the Lyons station where there is one
   train only, it full. She insists that her husband
   the doctor is needed, *officially* posted, must
   be allowed. Simone wants off the train—

   Mme. Weil says no.

5.   To be used in a dangerous mission—to join
     the Resistance: failure, her own,
     all of France's, shaming her; anger turning
     toward expiation. Obsessed with Arjuna's
     obligation to fight when yet he would not
     kill, in Marseilles she reads the *Gita*,
     begins to learn Sanskrit, to study God's action
     in Asian texts. Since she can't get out,
     in 1941, applying to teach.

                    Rejected. A Vichy decree
                    bars Jews from the professions.

6.   Arrested and threatened with the company of prostitutes
     in prison, Simone is overjoyed—not believing
     she should force herself on any person and not having,
     otherwise, any means for meeting women in this line.

                    Conviction overturned:
                    the judge finds her unstable.

7.   Coming back, to see Father Perrin—in the convent
     waiting all afternoon, she wants to talk about religion,
     believes there to be an insuperable obstacle
     to her conversion; still, she believes she is a person
     of *implicit faith, on the threshold of the Church.*

                    Rejected. Perrin: " . . . a real illusion
                    on her part. At first, she did not
                    seem to be aware of any problem. The love
                    of Christ seemed to be enough for her. Then,
                    she began to understand the doctrinal
                    depth of Catholicism . . . in all seriousness . . . ."

8. Winter-spring '42, in Marseilles she writes,
   I believe one identical thought is expressed precisely
   with slight differences of modality in
   >   *Pherekydes,*
   >   *Thales,*
   >   *Anaximander,*
   >   *Plato,*
   >   *Greek Stoics,*
   >   *Greek poetry of the great age,*
   >   *universal folklore,*
   >   *Upanishads,*
   >   *Bhagavad Gita,*
   >   *Chinese Taoist writings,*
   >   *certain currents of Buddhism,*
   >   *sacred writings of Egypt,*
   >   *Christian dogma,*
   >   *Christian mystics,*
   >   *some Christian heresies, Cathar, Manichaean, and*
   this thought today requires a modern and Western form
   of expression. That is to say, it requires to be expressed
   through the only approximately good thing we can call our own,
   namely science. This is all the less difficult because
   it is itself the origin of science.

   > Unread, then. Today rejected. Correctly,
   > as heretical; wrongly, as syncretic.

9. Places on a boat booked. *Am I running away?*
   But the Front Line Corps—would Americans? London?
   Seventeen days in Casablanca waiting to board
   the Portuguese steamer. July in New York
   on Riverside Drive. It is 1942.
   With her Plan she sets out— The Corps

              rejected, by Maritain, Washington,
              the Free French Committee,
              and the Free French Delegation.

10. A contact! Maurice Schumann, schoolmate, spokesman
    for Gaullists in London. Schumann shows the Plan
    to Commissioner Philip—

              he rejects it.
              He thinks he can use her.

11. Departure for London arranged. She arrives—is delayed
    for eighteen days in an internment camp. But *Here I am,*
    she says at last, *ready to sabotage—or, to organize.*

              Actually, Miss Weil,
              your desk is here.
              The committee proposals
              for postwar reconstruction,
              look them over—would you?
              Draw some, yourself.

12. *If you won't send me to sabotage, send me to spy.*
    Send me to some place we need to win at the cost
    of a life. I am here— Send me.

                    Rejected.

13. Fearing she fails in something commanded, failing
    to perform through lack of energy, faith, or power
    to persuade, for five months she asks to be sent,
    all the while working as an editor for Philip, generating
    proposals for the Free French; long hours, asleep
    at her desk, after the last train bent to her table;
    essays, reports, on the meaning of justice, the new
    Constitution, the colonial problem, the war;
    how inadequate Marxism is; how inadequate
    the doctrine of human personality. She writes about
    uprootedness and human obligation. For five
    months. Renewing her request.

                    Commissioner Philip: "Why doesn't she
                    concentrate on something concrete,
                    for instance trade union problems, instead
                    of remaining in generalities."

14. She asks to see a priest.

I can still hear Simone's voice in the deserted
streets of Marseilles as she accompanied
me to my hotel in the small hours. She was

commenting on the Gospel. Words issued
from her mouth as a tree yields its fruit.
Her words did not so much translate the truth

as pour it into me, whole and unadulterated.
I felt as if I were being transported
beyond space and time, so that I virtually fed

upon light. The systematic side of her work,
so weak and flat, intelligence in flashes
that can't be strung together. Not pearls.

HOW IMPERATIVES ENTER THE BODY

From a bed in Middlesex Hospital, concealing
her address, Simone is writing
to her mother . . . *my intelligence is praised*

as fools' foolishness is mocked, to evade
the question, Is what I speak the truth?
She asks to see a priest, who is "annoyed"

by her thought: it will not "grasp . . . itself
satisfactorily, and . . . [will] not accept fixed
starting points . . . ." It seems to him,

"too 'feminine' . . . too 'Judaic' . . . ." Her refusal
of treatment offends Dr. Bennett, who rules
her bed be given up, and she taken

to Kent, where they do not want her.
"We deal with industrial patients here
and feel she will not settle down with us."

JUSTICE

As justice is to disregard your strength in an unequal
        relationship and to treat the other
        in every detail, even intonation, posture, exactly

as an equal:
        so God

all-powerful, does not exert power; God waits like a beggar
        for us, made equal, Might drawn
        back

that the world
        be—

As justice: so God, secretly
        present, an opening in us that can move, consent, bond us
        forever,

but not
        appearing—appearing absent; except
        for how a thing can be beautiful, constrained

to its nature, how that
        snares us.

NECESSITY

If the sea should alter
the long movement of its waves
to spare a boat,

it would not be beautiful;
but being, at every point, obedient
to infinitesimal pressure of wind, water, light,

being nothing but
obedient, it moves us. We are moved
to venture

on it, not
because the sea will part
for us—

REVOLUTION: SIMONE AT 27

In Spain on the banks of the Ebro
as Durruti attacks Saragossa,
Simone speaks to peasants

and finds their feeling—sharp
inferiority—exacerbated
by the Revolution: militiamen

tyrannize an unarmed
population; she writes down
her own fear,

also, her lack of it: *how intensely*
everything around me
exists. War without prisoners—

lying on her back, rifle aimed
at the planes. Then she trips
into boiling oil buried in

a cooking pit: too scalded
to move. Silent, for weeks.
Bare, unconnected,

they come then, field-hospital accounts
of massacre, murder,
expeditions to kill Fascists

—*an elastic term,*
as she writes to Bernanos, *used*
for captured children shot.

By the fall of '36, the people's war
is over. She remembers Lenin
demanding a state

in which there would be neither
Army nor police nor a bureaucracy
distinct from the people;

but what emerged, after long civil war,
was a machine. The heaviest ever
laid on that people.

SOUL LEARNS EVERYTHING FROM BODY

The bird forgets,
        but the trap does not. Cassandran,
her harsh voice worrying, probing: *If any*
human being show need of any other, a little
or a lot, why does the latter run away?
I have much experience, on one side or the other.

Everything from the body:
                a boy
running down the field can *read* so well, his hands
are unimpeded, have already caught the pass;
reached out before
        he saw. Finally,
not to *read* at all: hands alone
fly up, whole body shaping the air, weaned, immediate.

The soul learns turning,
inclination,
fatigue:
to be worn down.

The body,
unastonished by reduction; it feels
what can be shown:
                that there exist remarkable
leafless trees of blossom,
                tiny
back and forth of almond, long, touched, wands of pink
that shudder down their whole length and are blown to the pavement

almost at once—

XERES: TAKE THIS CUP

It is said, she would allow one
of the nurses to wet her lips
with sherry, that her teeth

clenched when she spoke—
Finally the doctor gave in
and the order to feed her

by force was rescinded.
In a field not far from
the coroner's court

workmen prepared
a pauper grave;
for years

unmarked, save
by its plot
number.

YOUR DEATH: WHAT IS SAID

The *Kent Messenger* on Friday 3 September, 1943,
reported an inquest at Ashford on Professor Simone A. Weil,
34, late of the University of Paris *(sic)*. A woman doctor,
the senior medical officer at Grosvenor Sanatorium, said:

> "I tried to persuade Professor Weil to take some food
> and she said she would try. She did not
> eat, however, and gave as a reason
> the thought of her people in France starving."

The Coroner recorded suicide by starvation
"whilst the balance of her mind was disturbed."

    Equilibrium?

        The dove

when in free flight it beats the air and feels
that resistance might believe
it would fly even better
in the void—
       You say,
              the soul feels
hindered by its personality, desires it dissolved—
Imperiously wished. Like some flashpoint. Pouf!
through the trap-door.
A hermit wandering in the desert
found the Earthly Paradise. Figs as proof,
he went back to bring the brothers.
They persuaded him so gently,
no Macarius, no.

But you had no others,
no fellowship of Fathers.

Did you judge your death to be a more effective
witness than your life? If so,
you were correct
about us, we leap upon it to hold
against your work. By this
resistance, brought to keep them both

—your thought, your death—

in the mind, polar. There are days when I can see
one through the prism of the other.
The morning, before I went to work,
when my mother choked to death, my mother
who was starving herself,
they slid together.

Some part of me heard "dead" at once,
hissing forward, sucked
into the flesh, but the rest, I lag—
overshoot, begin a process,
false steps varying,
oscillating even, around

a wound I knew I had
received—

"Monster," is said. "Martyr." "Despair."

The words won't make it simple. Death rises
quite as you implied,
not only in the middle of a life,
but at the center.

She said,

when from the depth
of our being,
we need, we seek a sound

which does mean
something: when we cry out
for an answer,

and it is not granted, then,
we touch the silence
of God—

Some begin to talk,
to themselves, as do the mad;
some give

their hearts to silence.

TRUE NORTH

ON FIRST LOOKING INTO DIRINGER'S
THE ALPHABET: A KEY TO THE HISTORY OF MANKIND

I wanted . . . a *Guneaform*—a woman's form—of writing
and thought, perhaps, Cuneiform it, so tactile the script, palpable
wedges pressed in wet clay: writing "at once," as a fresco

is painted. But in this book, in the pictographs
that underlie Cuneiform, there is only one sign for woman,
pudendum. Slavegirl and male servant, also

given by genital description.
Man is head, with mouth in it, plus beard.
I thought apart from Diringer's claim, *origin* of alphabets,

this script is just one instance. Hieroglyphic
determinatives for man and woman in Egypt look more
matched, both stickfigure-like, both kneeling on one shin— Except

the woman has longer hair, no arms, no *difference* between
first- and second-person-singular. How quietly here ancient grammar states
what our marital law, or canon teaching on abortion, legislates:

"I am—not only yours—but you."
I began to wonder whether, somewhere in the world, different
thinking existed. Flipping through the book,

I was struck by Chinese trigrams, their elegant
abstraction: just three lines
above each other meant, the footnote said, sky and dry and prime

and creative: grandfather-life. Slashed, into six
little lines, the sign meant secondarily
and destruction, and foreboding, and grandmother, and earth.

Later Chinese for man, an upright stroke, hook rising to the left.
For woman, a buckling crook, large bundle at the shoulder.
Woman, next to woman, meaning quarrel—

and man, next to word, meaning *true*.
I did find toward the end one group of people, the Yao
or Miao, or Miao-tzu tribe, called

by the Chinese "wild Southern barbarians."
Fifty thousand in Vietnam and Laos before our war.
The Yao had, I found nowhere else, four

different signs of *equal* complication:
mother, father, person, heart
—but as I said, wiped out.

"A summer job in Waterbury, Connecticut, with the American Brass Company turned into a permanent one . . .

"I still have vivid sensual memories of that time: The smell of burning lard oil. Streams of molten brass in the casting shop. Some of the last coke-fired pit furnaces in operation, and men drawing crucibles, skimming and pouring the metal. The magnificent row of rolling mills, all driven continuously by a Corliss engine with a huge flywheel and a shaft running the full length of the large shop. The dance and clangor of drop and screw presses; and a sympathetic feeling for the pressure in the extrusion presses. Men seizing red-hot snakes of copper, threading them curving back and forth through the wire rod mill at Ansonia. (To this day a frequent dream is of wandering through complex assemblies of industrial buildings full of such machines, in search of something I never find.)

" . . . unlike the academic, who thinks his ideas seven days a week, as an industrial employee I had weekends free, and these enabled me to exploit the Sterling Library at nearby Yale University and develop my historical interests.

"World War II ended all this . . . . I went to Los Alamos to direct the work on metallurgy. This involved preparing the fissionable metal for the cores of the Hiroshima and Nagasaki bombs . . . .

"The work was applied science at its best . . . . The physical environment of mountains, mesa, and forest provided an inspiring backdrop . . . . It was a very different world from the Connecticut industrial town, and my intellectual horizons were tremendously widened as I found myself able to play a part in association with many of the greatest physicists of the time.

"Not only in the laboratory—I frequently went hiking in the mountains with Bethe, Fermi, Weisskopf, Teller, G.I. Taylor, and once even cajoled Johnny von Neumann into a short scramble up the Quemazon trail . . . .

All this served to intensify the intellectual slant of my mind that had been barely perceptible before, and it made the appeal of the intellectual world irresistible."

Cyril Stanley Smith
A Search For Structure
Cambridge, MA: MIT Press, 1981

CASTING OF BELLS GIVES WAY TO CASTING OF CANNON

Poles of knowing: Bell and Endor; one, a *theorem*,
one, a Witch of.

Saul and Macbeth, who both seek power beyond
what's possible, seek it through knowledge—a cult knowledge

retained in one Weird woman (after the countryside has been cleared
of women, who fly, who flew, who chatter

like wrens). What does the Witch teach? Only
what is: "Saul," she says, "give it up."

(But bred, punished, conditioned
into caution about home truth, how did she dare

to speak? All her sisters,
"cut off.") Bell's

theorem? The same. A frame for constraining. To the king's
desire, *Look into seeds of time and say which grows, which*

not, it says no
way is there to go a way not gone, no way to grow

(prognosticate) unchosen seed (untaken
paths), no going back on dice once cast, no *might-*

have-been that hangs around unless
it was: no *could*

but *is*. Poles set
a bound. Now, King (S(aul)/M(ac)),

they say, *Behold,*
Time rides, but time comes . . . .

TIME-CAPSULE CONTENTS

1   Sermon: *What Will Be Left?*

Weather, certainly. Even
the ticking earth must thaw. Genetic law

will prove to be present, each still-born defect
confirmation. Murmurous

why-lords, why this generation? This destruction
of our marrow. More than all

these, memory of Promise, her chrysalis
jeans, her eyes extraordinarily

bright, shadowed with
mascara: Honey,

as she was,
in heat, in bloom, in slow

motion, left, locked
in the projector.

2   Transcription of Outtakes from Pre-trial Deposition

I don't think flu
should be our *whole* answer.
Let's go over it, again.

Be more specific, if you can.
This record has to hold
up, for generations. We do know,

Colonel, you've been ill.
And you say, you were misled,
or did you say, unnerved,

by a woman selling apples
who tried to stop you
on your way to work.

You ordered, *Two* if by land,
you chose, *North* Dakota,
you swore, If your *right* hand

offend you— Is this
the statement, Sir, you wish
to give the court?

3   Journal Entry

In the shelter, I doze.
I remember
Indian October. An aquarium of birchleaves

flowing around us
slowly,
like nectar. Home loaves.

Dark oven. Syrup
on our fingers. Chrysanthemums
heavy, in the sugarbowl

of summer.

YOUNG WILLARD GIBBS IS A PHYSICIST

at home, in the home at High and Wall
he never left, his emotional life
"not fought for," Muriel said—

Rukeyser, who fought for his biography.
Self-appointed. Against her, cohorts
of colleagues and family who like Dickinson

kinsmen "Suffocate — with easy woe — "
all trace, all access to. Gibbs wasn't frail,
but strong. Not shy, presiding. At home

with ideas; not, with people—yet, if it were
important, he would praise: eulogizing
Clausius; if it were *very* important,

he would fight: over vectors, with Tait.
" . . . but I believe that there is a deeper
question of notions underlying

that of notations. Indeed, if my offence
had been solely in the matter
of notation . . . ."

Gibbs making found

    what lies hidden, so deeply nested
    is it within, so down
    deeply pocketed, miles

    from the icy, calm, notational
    surface: making a line,
    a lure, one symbol, one elliptical

    expression, holding echo
    upon echo, decoding
    to a catalog: an infinite

        acceptance . . .

detonation

    as almost welcome and always
    implicit
    in the mind, like the cloud, low,
    and going to snow

    in CT. Great still pool. Demoralized
    desire that waits for
    snow
    as if the snow were

        winged

HEAVEN AND EARTH, 1666

Copernicus

spoke more or less of the wander
of the earth and Mercury and Mars and the evening star
—which isn't a star—muttering,
"They do, they wander";

Tycho

the Dane kept scrupulous chart of that appearance;

Kepler

from Tycho's tables
drew laws that distressed him—*dung,*
he called them, looking for circles. Wonderful
laws: elongated curves of equal outsweep—elliptical
orbits—their speed increasing closing in on the Sun,
slowing down moving off, always the same
sweeping motion, Mercury, or Mars
or any of the wandering—

then *Newton*

                    saw
how it happened, how—Attraction!—their sped-up speed, their onrush
would come if the Sun were pulling on them, figuring
how
           strong a pull that might be, so weighing

           the sun,
and he,
young and the river flowing under him and the apple tree.

55

On your Mark, one first O/riginal Form; *Get set*, a second
angular Segment; *Go*—the next step, a Rule replacing
each straight side in the first by the second; if I take

a box and for each side of that box substitute a cone
or peak, to make a kind of star—then do *again*
what I did before: take the star-box

and where I find a straight-line replace it
with a peak, to make a *starrier* star, nesting the shape
even deeper in the figure, re-placing

peaks to make a Star-in-the-Box! Or, a Diamond-heart-
Star at *every* level (a shape self-similar); a shape
of extreme complication, in only a few—in five—

iterations, it already reads as texture and is rapidly
sinking as it plummets, repeating, into bonded
lock, where photons mediate, shunting between

heavy center, vibrant orbit. Or *deeper*, look. No,
look, a quantum leap: the burst box—the born star—is re-
emerging on the line, on the line *or/and* . . . . Repeat:

as myself—I act as the tongue
        of you," he said, or wrote: Walt Whitman. *Who?* Who *is*
                this massing, polled, this multi-point self?

"I showed her Heights she never saw —
        And now — 'Woulds't have me for a Guest?'
                She could not find her Yes — "

Dickinson wrote. Then
        re-wrote, *as*
                "He showed me heights I never saw — "

Deeper
        duplicity: none. Role, trope, and object: all
                reversing, as if all were one

affair—
        of language.
                Cooing,

the bird outside my window takes no notice,
        mid-morning or dawn or supper, it is mournful: *Oh but—who-*
                who-who the form of its floating

sorrow, so intent
        and equable now in its sorrow, so patient
                and outbreathing

now, of its sorrow. I had
        hoped to find the iris tended
                still, in Gibbs's garden; I thought women

of that town, if they had
        a garden club, or League, would come with dark blue
            bulbs

or yellow-tongued; I thought they would keep
        a Garden, but
            they tore it

limb from limb, beheading, dripping, tore the house
        on High
            Street down.

IRIS AN ILLUSION

Consider
        the ink-charged brush
on Wang Wei's scroll, how the stroke that will mean tree
is nothing like the one for river, though all

is smoke here, barely visible
        plumes and patches: carbon particles of ink
bleeding a border, according to competing capillarities
of fiber in the brush,

the paper. Consider
        the stroke, how it is part of the hill, part
of the middle ground of this scroll from *The White Crane*
series, said to be in Wang Wei's style: repetitions

of direction
        —the roof tiles, say, "echoing" branches;
mountain valleys wrinkled, like rock fissure—
angles of juncture at points on the scroll, not themselves

interlocked there, lock inside
        the rapt observer, who gazes not over
but in and out, now seeing, now not,
an arc in the mist

film will capture,
        though we can't. Call
the rainbow *illusion,* then—
but

gasp
        as that huge fish *in one shimmering*
bound clears the vault, eludes
grasp.

REAL TOADS

Dreamlike as the garden was, full—filling—
as it was
with trysts, wisteria, murmurs to interpret; Heaven-Pattern
of assassins
as it turned out it was, a place with one Namer,
two trees, four speakers sinuously
blaming: *only* dreaming
could have made Him make it, dream solution, Mother-
of-Dream dyeing His brain so deeply green
He moaned and woke—to find it outside Him,
an abrupt project,
landscape: *green-er-y*. Not for that,
less wholly dream; it was dream
to the core,
His garden, His greenness.

In it, badger, smoke, time—orderless creatures. Time,
a creature He tried to annihilate; time,
a badger, big-bellied, awkward, lifting
her head, catching a scent. She backed down
from her branch, slipped her paws in the stream
where His thought flashed in schools, as if scavenging
a minnow, the glint of a pebble, and the stream
grew turbid, its waters went backward
and all they carried, backward, the swill,
the silt: all the dead,
fouling the water, until He repented
even what had come
unbidden, even what He hadn't
dreamed. Still
she stirred.

He repented repenting. He choked in His thought,
in faces of the dead. Livid, rose
from His sleeplessness. To escape these dead
broke into His own dream,
hoping for refuge; found it not the same thing
He adored, waking: the crystallized
green thing. Feared
that difference. Feared
those dead.

To each gate where He'd set a turning angel with cesium sword
and red glass eyes that lit and unlit, He returned
to pull the circuit. Thought again. Went back
again and smashed the angel's
hand, which was a coinbox. Dimes
spurted from the jagged thumb
against the gate, on
the concrete.

In the sudden un-angeled quiet, old sinews, lost tongues, quit gripping
the wall of the cave where they'd hidden; hearing silence
at the entrance, they let go, lengthened. One—or two
whole bodies tumbled from the sky, and crumpled fingers
in loose enough soil pushed up like fescue,
all pale, all stunted. In clumps,
like women or workmen, very few together.
Each, amazed at the surface of the earth, even lying down
and laughing, not too loudly.
The palms held grass blades
to the lips, and the lips whistled—
as if that were enough; as if

what the eyes saw were only
a blindness
eyes are subject
to;

this is what the eyes knew: how close to abortive
such birth was; how time had no way
to parlay a gain, or even repeat it;
how time and the animals were
not allied; how,

already, on the charged horizon,
the odds
had risen too high.

AMERICAN SPEECH

Resistance to tyrants *is* obedience to God.
      Don't Tread On Me!
            The Connecticut Valley

has to be
      the most
            abstract location in the universe——minds

of winter, minds of Iceland spar, at work
      in Dickinson, Edwards,
            Peirce,

and Gibbs. The whole a hotbed
      of revival, of Great Awakening: the one
            word

Noah Webster invented, of all those
      in his book,
            demoralise,

a slow
      seep into melting snow and gray afternoon;
            Gibby, skating

long strokes on the pond; Emily
      watching freedom
            condense

inside the clear glass of her window.
      In this Valley, neighbors
            disregard

—sustain—hidden fervence, run Underground
　　　railroads; *Images and Shadows*
　　　　　sewn up

in Edwards's notebooks, flint
　　　stitched into Dickinson's, 700
　　　　　equations

of Gibbs's great paper set up in type at last
　　　by shopkeepers'
　　　　　subscription: in CT, they

Make Do, but they tore
　　　the house, the home on High Street, Gibbs's—born
　　　　　and died there—down.

JUS SUUM: WHAT CAN NEVER BE TAKEN

JOSIAH WILLARD GIBBS, 1790–1861

. . . that the *question*
can be tolerated—whether they be

freemen—for
a single moment, Gibbs said

(Josiah Willard the Elder, Professor at Yale
of sacred books). *Language*

is a cast of the human mind
Gibbs Elder said, visiting the jail

in 1839, to give theirs back
to them, on "our" soil: transcribing

sounds, for words
for numbers, told to him

from behind their bars
when he held up his fingers: 1, 2, . . . 5, . . . 10;

then traveling to New York, by stagecoach,
ship, to the port, to seek—and find,

on a British brig, someone who spoke
Mendi *and* English,

that African men, Black mutineers,
might claim their right—should they

have had to? Inalienable—
in an American court,

convened in Connecticut, *New Haven,*
where the slaveship was tied up.

Our courts,
he said. The shame

to our courts, that the question could be tolerated
(whether

they be freemen—regaining their freedom—
or criminals, or property)

for a single

moment.

HOLDING THE OTHER HOSTAGE

How the opposed breed each other, cast
and mold they *are* one boundary, all

inversions re-inforce for between them
they rule: they rule out. They cleave

together and better than love are
righteously cruel: white Slave-

holding Mistress. Their epithets mean
you are strangely polluted, you

immigrant Alien, Jew, Gentile
dog. How to change their success? Change

the neighborhood. Change what you call
"dark"; I, "intimate." Control means to hold

the *contre-rôle,* the duplicate register.
What of the night? Who knits there?

ARTICULATE AMONG US

EMILY ELIZABETH DICKINSON, 1830–1886
JOSIAH WILLARD GIBBS, 1839–1903

Never married, never moved from their Family Home.

I am so potent, I can reach you only after wave upon wave
of dilution. You will re-discover, but not read me.
I have built a language to make my work more pure.

A pure inquiry—into unity—has concerned this nation
ever since it claimed Independence through union. Cornerstones
of the Church on the Green in New Haven, monuments

to Regicide: Dickinson a Fire Bride, a bomb, a volcano. As alive,
or more so, in the grave as out of it. Showing us this across the garden
fence of the grave. Speaking in the tomb, of the tomb, as of a ride,

one of many, every poem one of many, No-name inquiries—
but we have her numbered. *Is* Dickinson articulate? Did Higginson,
Johnson, Franklin—would Bloom, if Bloom spoke of her—make her

articulate? She said the grave gave her language.
Whitman said the future, always sampling the future, enlisting the future,
and Gibbs a prisoner, of his own unwillingness to auction

his mind, who built a mathematic language to make his work *more pure*—
who made it so pure it sublimed instantly into zones of power
and remains enthroned there, isolated there. The supremely

articulate among us, *Amistad* Africans, mutineers for freedom
on the ship they commandeered, stole from the captain and steered
by their own light—and by starlight—to a New World, a rock-bound

coast; a world not wilderness alone but Wilderness with courts
in it, and canon, and codes of presentation, a world of sacred
language their own language attacked, active virus, ancient

knowledge that it was, *they* perplex— No translator.
No way-maker. No wizard wise woman sponsor. Only the Valley
itself of the Connecticut River, who brought from itself,

with the help of Sarah, Jonathan Edwards. A valley
itself with its snow and snow water. So far from Home.

> *I am so potent, I can reach you only by submitting*
> *to wave upon wave of dilution. So potent*
> *only I can reach you: now. Soon.*

REAL LIFE IS WHITE IN CONNECTICUT

pale green
and white in Connecticut trees elms The Common
the sky the mind in Connecticut calcite bar
of burning crystal prism on the sill

       iris in the garden
       charts and charters
       sea-bitten shore

permitting oneself little that little cold
sharp as bramblepoints in air seeded with new snow
to come in Connecticut outpouring down pouring
crystals to come full of the hint and intimation
of snow the overwhelming darkening white of the snow
burying bodies in CT blinding angled sheet of its softness
biting at the shore of the sky

iris—itself—short sword in the pale
green spring of CT unassuming
terse

       April snow
       stained by flowers

TRUE NORTH 3

It's Hard

The noontime shadow changes length very slowly.
The noontime shadow is only *one* length: its length at noon.
The noontime shadow—my watch

is usually off, anyway. It's hard—I mean, it's difficult
what with the little ridges in the dust,
the cellophane-silvery

glare on the sand, trying to track it over
those few moments. It was getting shorter: that much was clear,
that part was easy. And then,

it dawns
on you, or dusks, getting longer
again, yes, indubitably;

but that zone, that zero, that anxiety
of getting it just, so, at its very
consensual

shortest: things are changing
now, here, so minutely, with such delicacy, North,
and noon, and this sort

of wonderful
vertical
stick.

O SHORTCUT TO WHAT?

O   *Nothing that is not there and the nothing that is.*
                     WALLACE STEVENS, "THE SNOW MAN"

Out the door every
day along High Street
to Sloane. Only the grave
there still and the grave gates, Egyptian
red soft sandstone. Every
day. Truth not flowing down
from a source; but, an exact
accord that makes the whole
simpler than the parts;
those bodies lost all winter
in the snow. The storm
in the night so great,
so erasing the man

so immemorably standing in it, at sea in it,
and the woman in batiste weeds of white at sea
in it on her widowed watching walk.

Gibbs spoke only once
in a Faculty Meeting, during
protracted, tiring debate on elective courses:
should there be—more English, more Classics? More? Or less.
They were astonished to see him rise, after thirty-two years,
though familiar with the high, pained-sounding voice: a man of snow
assessing. Not to be distracted, or dispersed into longcuts,
not to be turned from the whole entire empty mist
hanging in the cold air, not to miss—or
intrude on the nothing that was
there.

Escaping,
in every emotional way,

Gibbs, hidden at home, creating the loneliness
he needed to assume just one responsibility—for which no thanks,
much complaining of it, some wonder. Lost, in the clouds of snow gathering
in CT over *Transactions & Proceedings* of the local Academy of Sciences,
the one un-evasion he accepted: shortcutting elegance by uncouth
statement that is efficient in every respect. The reward for
getting past the failings of language? To be found
un-readable. Gibbs rose. He said: *Mathematics
is a language*. And sat down.

(()

The Silver Power
of Zero makes a mirror-

realm: *Are-not*.
Domain

trails from itself the ink
Minus, sign of Debt,

of Doubt, of Double-
entry: books to keep

or doubled sets
of points to win. *Zero-*

sum? Of two,
one wins. Only one.

(((( )))

The need to write down numbers: not some, but All,

and I can do it—and I do, euphoric, disquiet— All is smaller
than few by far by Far, a series summed, a limit
passed-to and subsumed, itself now item;

a method: for Truth, which means here

depth, the Peirce-ing range, the finer mesh, the even deeper
reach through layer into layer holding
up: still true, still *truer*. Not logical, not only;

the truth of a ravening child who must find

divinity Exact—exactly to find it: Pythagoras stopped
and offered sacrifice to God when he discovered
that the circle was

a locus of means. Far-seer. Canny conceiver. With a snake

in his pocket, but ravenous, retreating from few
to All, to four corners of the wind, of the world
turning gold, gold as corn and pumpkin. Gold as control.

5 (IMAGINARY NUMBERS)

(IM   (RE (RA   (IN   (NA   ))))

I spell it out—
                    to spell it in; I cast a spell
        that puts an end
to all distinction: more including, wider flung, closer spun, more pen-
etrant, or more in-
        fusing, if we only knew what
empty space was—the solid part of a table *one* part in each Quadrillion:
        Im Re.Rainna: Im Re.writing the Imaginary
Natural Integral Rational Real

                    as

Identical. Crimson. 5. Uprising droplet petals
        resist
                    disappearance, de-
vitrify: star at the skin
and grow
inward in the form
of
        Iota:

                    Iota
                    and her anti-self
                    cancel: Iota,
                    dividing herself, is still
                    hidden: none,
                    but one; but Iota,[+]
                    returned to herself, overlaying
                    herself, an enfolding

[+] $(-1)^{1/2}$

76

Revelation
of One who-is-and-is-not-one, who is Not-one, who
returned
to herself is real, and Minus: rotational
Spine
—Girder and
Axis
of description in the
(actual) quantum
mechanical
world, in the
Body
Electric.

WHO,

then, sweeps
them loose, who diffuses

broken, shining bits, the farflung force
washed to foam on a rockface, succulents

and whelks alive inside
its razing spray? Who slings

the broth aslide in cups of ocean swell? Whose bolt
of lace, a great spill of it blowing

in the window with her pins, patterns the firmament, patterns
the phosphorescent body of an Eel making slip-knots

in the dark sea, patterns fireflies sailing
through grass at the edge

of a wood, lit—and unlit—at twilight, giving
body to the air,

or to some, brimming, being
—whose? Who?

HAG OF BEARE, OR THE CALENDAR GIRL

As Ancient forests, turned to black blood
by the weight of the earth, are put alight

by the rocket's glare, by the Brilliant Bombs
bursting red in the bitter air, a Cockpit womb

exploding there, the Challenger
in fiery flight, the Hag of Beare

burning in air, the sea itself set afire by night
will turn on the earth, will hold its waves

coherent, drone one wailing dirge—one gathering might
will surge away from the vortices, the hissing cry

of little wheels and one wall rise, one shrug, one massing
watery wall—no breaking fall, no broken power,

no canceling phase, but racing its way
and gaining speed in straits at the Drake

for towering miles: implacable tons of frozen
hollow watery boom erase green earth, dislodge the moon

from fragile orbit: flame and slag the meteoric
womb of moon come hurtling down—

the flying broom a woman rode, a woman alone
at her sweeping work, saving leavings,

accounted prayer, reckoning remnant patch
and scrap, leastings, faintly floating webs

of star-drift, woman aligned with a Goose,
astride the Mother who navigates, who flies

in formation though skies are falling,
who flies though the Poles themselves

aren't fixed—what Cup, what Broom,
what Web, what Term? Over

the rainbow? Open
sky? A moveable home—to none

denied? With you. With you.
By—and by.

NARROWNESS OF NARROW PATH ENDURED

Identical in nature, but differing
in phase, are we at odds? Can we be contained
on a riling, ruthlessly captained, single ship?

It swirls like a stick in the whirlpool at the Straits.

Can we be controlled by a motherly gaze? By the tottering
walk of a mother-to-be who caresses the already-born
with eyes and tongue, but self-absorbed

in the one-to-come, sways as she walks catching the sun

on one shoulder, then another, perambulating mother?
Or by him, one of the roughs, melding
with the crowd—with them all, but untouched?

Can we be compassed by thought? "Let us imagine,"

said Gibbs, abstracting pure Rule,[+] that will fuel
the Third Reich, "a great number of independent
systems . . . ." Most certainly at odds. Most certainly competing.

Can they be assessed? In a lab? At a desk? Can they

be changed? By a go-between? With their disastrous
capability of relaxing the entire, the major, the inherent
interconnection of this extended system back . . . to

snow, to fall-out in the dark, to frozen

[+] The Phase Rule.

rock surrounded by black pine, back-lit by the enormity of
no-longer-starlight illumining the dance
of a ghostly dancer—highwayman

in the snow, who longing to see her dance, exposed,

waylays, waylaid her. O little girls, with your babble
and braids, putting raincoats on the babies, talking
the toddlers out of fright

at the lightning, one of you shinnying the radiator pole—

one, with bursting cheeks; you older girls, not allowing
cursing on the landing, where all seek shelter
from the sudden summer storm: not

yet the prolonged voluptuous seen—and reseen—reseen

rescene: immolating stormflight of the young motherteacher
burned again and again before the eyes of her daughter
and her son; not narrow enough, the path of control,

Canaveral, Chernobyl— Not narrow, at all.

TRUE NORTH 5

It's Easy

at the South Pole. There *every*
direction
is true North. Direction, there, itself

the point
turning and moving,
or the place

where you look, if you still
stand waiting.
Though

you forget
all the steps—forget!
Remember,

every,
and so *easy*,
at

the nadir.

V : WAVESON.NETS / LOSING L'UNA

LOSING L'UNA

ERRAND UPON WHICH WE CAME

7.113

Gentle Reader, begin anywhere. Skip anything. This text
is framed
fully for the purposes of skipping. Of course,

7.114

it can
be read straight through, but this is not a better reading,
not a better life. You are being asked

7.115

to move with great
rapidity. As if it weren't there. As if you were a frog,
a frog that since it's disappearing

7.116

thinks to ask,
for the first time, in which element it really does
belong. Leaping progress

7.117

will consist
in considering this and closing the book. Anything
else will represent a settled course.

7.118

Indeed, it is true that much has fallen
through the cracks,
but the most painstaking and willful path

7.119

will not recover this (recoverable?)
material any better
at all than the soft ziggy sampling butterfly approach.

7.120

Gentle Reader,
who labors, who tugs up roots to get beyond roots
—as it were—do roots entwingle

7.121

space? Where do we mine that knowledge
of what cannot be precipitous, nor yet
delayed?

7.122

What if the go(o)ds refuse
to go
to market? What then?

7.123

Will is broken by the trials of all folktales, the Augean stables,
the straw spun. A nail
that fixes the center so the register is true—

7.124

what the scale hangs on,
not what
the pointer points to.

FROM SAILS TO SATELLITES

1.26

From Sails to Satellites, J. E. D. Williams, reviewed in *The Sciences*, Jan/Feb 1994, p. 51:

" . . . even Williams, who surely must derive comfort from
the ease of contemporary navigational methods, senses that
something has been lost with the passing of the sextant and
the chronometer. Navigation has become a matter of numbers,
whereas once it was a way of apprehending one's place in the
cosmos. Williams recalls one long flight across the Atlantic, on
which, plagued by radio failure, he was forced to shoot the stars
to determine his flight path. Clouds stretched below him in an
unbroken sheet, obscuring the marine light that would have
marked the African coast. But, as Williams remembers, 'when
we broke cloud and there was the light, exactly where it should
have been, the sensation was more of harmony with the universe
than satisfaction with oneself. A computer display is not the
same thing.'"

1.27

A universe
meets the hand that pushes against it
in the form of

1.28

a limit
that it pushes up against, or seeks
to circumvent; it rewards

1.29

a hand-mind that reaches for
its breast, a mouth not
held back,

1.30

by pattern upon pattern giving way to deeper
grasp giving in to rhythm or
vibration or milk.

EVIL IS EXTERNAL

1

Evil is external to itself: where it is, it is not felt.
It is felt where it is not: the feeling
of evil is not

2

evil.
Where it is: the God-blaming criminal;
where it is not:

3

a woman
feeling in her body what the rapist denies,
denies hoarding, denies passing on, because

4

he does not feel it. She
feels it. The whole weight of his force
and his forgetfulness;

5

it stops with her. It stops her.
No one wants to see it. To see it is against
the soul's

6

aspiration, *ergo* she is beaten.
Or killed—
or stoned or shunned.

3.43

Cut the ring in half—she still insists
on the *roughness*
of the divide: "body," "body" slash

3.44

"what"?
What you jump at,
shy at. Bristle at.

3.45

Water's pliant attentiveness,
the negative trial: not to eat a fruit,
not pomegranate, not apple;

3.46

not to open a door,
nor the lid of a box, not to think
about the white bear, not to look

3.47

upon
him, naked;
Kore, Pandora, Psyche, Eve, Briar Red, Snow White,

3.48

what is infinite
in doing is don't
ever: the taboo, the *geas*.

3.49

Simone, when you leapt, angled barbs on the fence
tore your scalp and you kept
rubbing blood from your eyes and stared and wouldn't

3.50

lie down,
or when the branches you barged through flooded you
with petals, white, wet, more softness

3.51

than you could shake off, you gave
no ground. Tines of lightning split
the tree: inside, creamy

3.52

and yellow. Your eyes brightened only
as the storm shifted, colder, harder, less
lurid. A word

3.53

can drain your cheek.
The lips of your wound begin to mend, but heal badly,
a welt, discolored, brown

3.54

as dogwood petals knocked to the ground
notched with crimson
as if blood flecked the wind.

WEARING OUT

1

Your canvas shoes wore out. You refused
to buy others. So when Thibon
got you work

2

in the arbor, somebody gave you
old sabots.
The strap gnawed your ankle.

3

You kept pace. Never behind
by a single plant. "Pluck!"
the harvest-master said.

4

World at war.
Glasses.
Shoes.

4·55

Assured, or cocksure? Astounding, her
severity of judgment. Preaching
neither love nor virtue, she traded in money,

4·56

ration books, coal, lodging, instruction, help
with job-seeking, passports, citizenship
& testimony.

4·57

A paralyzing deep-seated sense
of ineffectiveness coexists
with hyperactivity and apparent over-confidence, as

4·58

the clinical text says. Perhaps. But to learn
"they" come from *tight-knit*
non-fighting families prone to conflict-avoidance

4·59

and live out the remarks made about them . . . well,
some, maybe all, bodies resonate
to others' spoken words, but here, it seems,

4.60

words eaten. And re-heard. *The anorexic*
feels herself to be a victim
of nicknames, of wrong labeling.

4.61

To call Olbers' Paradox *Olbers'*
Paradox is wrong labeling. Miss Gingerbread
Dickinson is wrong labeling, unless we imagine her

4.62

indeed a witch, *maîtresse* of a sugar house
she baked which did not melt
around its own oven, sensing she must court

4.63

the children of the place. Stein
(as opposed to Gerty M.) barely able
to be labeled—as she engineered—

4.64

but a lot of "wrong" fluster and not
anorexic; so, perhaps, too *broad* a cause,
one must pause before relying on it.

4.65

For an anorexic, an autonomous woman is
a contradiction in terms. Whereas,
for Simone, "decisiveness" exists in the privileged

4.66

castes. Others come to see it as a truth and fact
of nature. And *she* came to see it, who knew
it wasn't so, temporarily immersed

4.67

in the work of those
others; she, too, eviscerated; entitlement lost
in a practice that occurred directly

4.68

on her body, scheduling her body. "Qualities
I thought my own, of my mind, were removed
inside one hour on the factory floor."

4.69

Why struggle to combat affliction?
In order, she answered, to restore the false
sense of a rightful self to every person

4.70

that they might make the only significant
choice open to them, *how* to renounce it
again, turn or not turn, leap—or stay; but since

4.71

it is the only choice, the only *human* thing,
the conditions of a full life being the same
for all human beings, our vocation

4.72

in the world *is* to restore the sense
of a rightful self to those deprived of it. To all,
that is. You and your partner, in every

4.73

interaction, restore,
or defeat.
Tertium non datur. Simone

4.74

was acute. Stein dark and sparkling. Money
was prominent in their writings,
and how wealth grows and families, and peoples,

4.75

and "pleasant family life," and one's native
language: roots of every sort. That knowledge
thrown up in a person kept apart, then

4.76

displaced, then again driven out—of her refugee
country, on her third reversal of fortune,
and so forth. Weil advised De Gaulle

4.77

to free Algeria: Antigone,
defeated, echoing Cassandra's wail—
our firebrand brother, Paris,

4.78

burns us all. *Aii-eeee!*
she said, do you know with *whom*
you deal? Or the stake? Or *how* they are called?

L'UNA LOSES

0.0

Moon over Manhattan.
Moon over Dover.
Moon over

0.1

the London-Dover train,
over bed 104, almost at the intersection
of two wings,

0.2

moon over the meadows
of St. Jean de Lalandes
where she had pitched hay,

0.3

over Carron de Gron
where she worked
beetroot fields,

0.4

St. Julien-de-Peyrolas
whose grapes
she had picked stretched out on the ground.

0.5

The danger not
that I should doubt whether there is
any bread, but that, by a lie,

0.6

I should persuade myself that I am not hungry.
It was a different set of wars.
Configuration is not statement.

0.7

The invisible pole, although she does not
write it—only twice
referring to it,

0.8

boats unloading at the dock—that would be 1942.
Reciting another's text. One pole.
And the other, Jardin du Luxembourg.

0.9

Another's text: *Taste my meat.*
Occupation: *Rédacteur (C.F.N.L.)*
Religion: too ill

0.10

to be examined properly.
Weight on admission:
stretcher case.

0.11

The painful struggle
about her light began all over
again. L'una eaten by night,

0.12

by sun, by war,
by the sequence of events in an ordeal,
or quest,

0.11

yet what did she seek? *The reality
my inattentiveness
screened*. Now sinking

0.10

all the time.
*But soon I will no longer be
cut out.*

0.9

To deny the opposition, "good" slash "evil,"
she said, use Irreligion: no difference between them—
or Idolatry, force supersedes

0.8

them; a third
way, to mute this opposition
occurs in the Gospels,

0.7

a way of living based on obligation, a concrete
way
of placing the body, grounding

0.6

violent
apprenticeship—
Tuesday

0.5

night.
At half-past ten.
Loss, she said, is the heart

0.4

of gambling.
L'una
loses. Luminous, lingering, dropping

0.3

her net, her cut
spool of star-
stained ocean, Channel foam, the Roman

0.2

sea, cliffs of Manhattan.
I will be added and united.
Failing, falling

0.1

behind,
below, inside, the crashing, faintly
smoking surf, she

0.0

fades
to day, to dawn, to
gone, to Dis-

o

appeared.

V : WAVESON.NETS / LOSING L'UNA

WAVESON.NETS

If you understand virginity,
you understand abstraction, you understand V—
V which is flight, and you understand VVV,
i.e., ric-rac, the earliest recorded

symbolic motif, Cassiopeian breasts pouring forth
a Milky Way, a.k.a. zigzag,
world-over water, meander, serpentine
cupmark U adjoining its inverse, upsidedown

U (please imagine), yourself
optimizing, as you do not lift but leave
your point (become pointed) pressed hard
to bone to pull that bone

writhing on your point, twist it one way,
then the other—a rhythm method making
your water mark.

If you understand red, you understand ruby,
you understand light bubbling up struck seam
first morning cliff; you do not
mock the real

as you watch it subside and divide and then run
like morning into the virtual.
If you understand vulva, you understand lens,
you understand an entrance

to unsuspected, fertile, labyrinthine darkness,
the power of ex-opponents or logs. If you put
your meander/zigzag/ric-rac
on your fabricated lens-shape, if indeed you dip

your lens into water and discover that the water
you meant to mark the lens with as a sign
of vulval moisture

is itself a lens, this clear drop beading up
on your lens stone, and you can see through it
to a life in the stone, to a depth
you did not suspect, do you bother to go back

to your old ox-head, its uterine face,
its Fallopian horns, to mark them
with meander, once you have discovered
wells open at the bottom leading to the next world,

wormholes, keyholes, the high
road to heaven, the flying carpet, the cataract?
You might. You might
go back,

stunned—for you no longer live
but rather remember what is a suddenly long-ago
childhood: marks

as marks, flesh as flesh,
their secrets those of separate realms.
Back then, a diagrammed
circuit *not* a circuit, as it is, now,

incised by the woman's, or the robotic,
"hand" on the golden wafer
in the virginally pure and guarded
clean room, eye to lens, as she makes her

—but whose?—meander mark.
If you understand virginity,
you understand abstraction and all there is to know
of immaculate, conception.

If you understood red, but—you cannot;
for you understand web
glistening in sunlight as stronger than steel

per ounce. You attempt to reverse engineer it
as you once calibrated the magnification achieved
by a dewdrop, compelled,
and even soothed;

but if you understood ruby, the haunted road
of a human
voice, complex waveform
not (by the ear) disassembled, not

processed in separate
recordings, followed on
by component reunitings, no *visual* mix, but all fused
into one

vibration received by one membrane,
the eardrum . . . porous . . . heard herald world
of word shaped.

He now let the animals name *him*.
He played tag with them
and was vanquished by touch.
As she wove her seven-bristled,

quarter-circle broom,
as she told the days to parturition, did she curse
the most time-taking
way, the straight

path, the unaccelerated route?
Playing cat's
cradle with the V, wedging the gap,
corking

the grail, that bottle of time too soon
spilled out. Left to itself,
in tidal flows,

there would be no tomorrow.
She craves that drift.
But this is her
primordial

task, to keep time, to serve it, an order
learned from the water bird
who makes a 3-prong
Y print

in the sand, echoed each time she stands
in trembling waves.
A cast
shadow, a thrown reflection,

and a subtly bent refraction
where the water meets the sky
and the land, 3 axes, and a mapping,

and 5, she mapped, who veers
as she flies, who carries the tilted earth
on her back. This is hallucinated hearing
in the service of art, of Arthur's table,

R2, Artemis,
and Ursa guarding the Pole.
Welcome, then, Presence, Reflection, Shadow,
Refraction, She Who Stands,

Gnova, Gnomon, Goose, Ouzel, Orca, Longdark,
Hardware, Software, Wetware, a Dolphin
leaping, responding
to the bare boy on her back.

For a crown is a cradle.
Wings are conical baskets of grain, baskets of fish
slung from her shoulders.

Screech owl nailed to the barnhouse door,
blows raining down on her,
fagots heaped. The persecutor's desire
to see,

as he sets the ordeal. What has happened? All
participate: sabbat.
Freud to Fleiss, 1897, is speaking about
The Witch Fixer, Hexenhammer,

in Latin, *Malleus Maleficarum,* the work of two monks,
themselves German. "The medieval theory
of possession," Freud writes, "upheld by ecclesiastical
tribunals is identical to our theory . . .

why do confessions extorted by torture bear so
much resemblance to my
patients' narratives during treatment?"

Some see the strong *fiat* as hopelessly strong
and steel their mind to it.
Some see nothing, happenstance, confusion.
At the quantum, basis of all that is stable,

numeric and morphic play with each other.
Not whether, but when: each level within
the atom, a pattern of resonant lock—
and each one without.

Hard steel punch. Soft silver being chased.
Everything you taste, or hear, or touch,
has a kind of limit, in response to stress,
beyond which relaxation is . . . to . . . something

other.
Loss of core memory.
Erasure.

ZONE : ZERO

CONSTANT QUIET

constant quiet
        intercostal
                intercoastal green *&* silver
                muscled gillflesh slipping into
        opens out of
constant quiet

constant quiet
        Mississippi
                overflowing built a levee
                longer higher than the Great
        Wall of China
constant quiet

constant quiet
        building building
                horse paunch pistol man
                long back cropper convict
        steel muscled
constant quiet

constant quiet
        longer higher
                than the Great Wall of China
                Egypt Mississippi hunger
        flogged
constant quiet

constant quiet
      storm of air
            ocean storms
            River rising
     field gone train gone man gone
constant quiet

constant quiet
      who can open
            who can
            hold it
     constant
quiet

holy war to keep the sun moving a sacrifice process jaw jaw mother sweep the floor	
	never go anywhere bliss so much flows by not sea or sky no woman no cry
mystic immersion enabled smite embedding enabled	
	on deck before he didn't know it death old football yarns
so tensely forgot Plum Creek to Plum Island spent fuel rocks	
	the green and white alabaster city of ancient glowing lamps
pyre at the river ember-eyed stranger strangling net of his abundant hair	
	cartoons graphing statistics videophone . . . lag . . . br eak i ng up

Discovery Channel gladiator slave awarded wooden freedom sword refusing it to plunge back into sex star status	
	the mammoth virgin in Athens or Nashville her hugely plated body dress Fort Knox
answering armswing of the moon ink ocean green scope	
	sampling *of mass* genetic *destruction* algorithm *weapons* recombine
ghost nets hollow the sea Occidio pink acid cloud	
	Sukey and Noose get it on— no more fairy thorn
the nectar thus freed malarial pool leprosarial pox scrotal basketballs	
	hand to elbow and slate write erase write erase

tactician's dream logistician's nightmare incapable silk underpants between them	
	both the *Half-Life* and *Quake* game engines may be used in this way
put out the all-seeing eye yours mine deputized counter	
	let through the crystal the changing state selected by collapse
pulverized by Desert Shield the desert's shield of pebbles that had held down pillar billow plume	
	naked eye the Beehive a dim mist on a clear night
cipher *sifr* o ease and flow 1 2 3 apricot albricoque *al-birquq*	
	once met once they have met spatial separation does not divide them

OPEN CAGE

To forget what has happened is a sacrament, an access
of power: the furor of these bronze leaves helpless to surround
a shrieking

ball of birdsong
gathered underneath towering
cauldrons of gold.

For nothing do you grieve. They twitter, the sound
careening like curraghs on unnavigable water. *Nothing.*
Clamor. The wind dies down. Memory

gone
visibly burning in the gold sea of the air,
cinders drifting on the black gold of the ground.

BALLAD OF SAND AND HARRY SOOT

0

Sand was a gourd fanatic
and she played
a glass
marimba.

I

Harry Soot loved to listen.

0

When Sand shook,
a green ribbon of rainsound
rose and fell in the air,

and when she let her mallet
fall, the palest of violets, a screen of violet
silver unscrolled.

I

Soot ground his keys
in his pocket,
defacing his MetroCard.

o

Should Sand sing,

I

       Harry felt himself leaning over a piano
              loosening his tie. As he reached out
       his hand, it was as if the inside of seventeen
       stretched balloons expanded past ivory,
       past gray, past transparence. A single spot,
       hung from the chrome scaffolding, bore
            down
       on the hoof of his nail.

o

Sand had a wardrobe
made of twirlies.

I

       Harry Soot
       tried to find a center. Beneath or beyond.
       A point to yield or resist.
       Liquefaction of furbelows.
       Buglebead ballast. Contour cups
         of constructed silk.
       A skein that flung itself into a cusp of droplets.

I

Harry Soot was a handsome man,
woody and gaunt.
A blue-eyed boy.

o

Sand well Sand was hard to say.
Some saw horns. Some saw
    slidebars. All
saw pointers
    but acknowledged them diversions.
A dragon, perhaps.

                    Or a dragon
        meditation?

o

Sand panned speed. Languid was she. Oh seeming fast, fine foil for
de . . . lay, lo, slow. Some slipp . . . age, she . . .

    I

    He, Harry, hurried, harried host.

o

Sand's similarity to scarabs?
Or a *rosa dolorosa*, every petal
thorned? Or swallows up close.
"The tail is forked and as elegant
as a trout's, but more attenuated,
just short of baroque," says the
naturist. I quote.

I

Harry succinct long gone
to the lake with his tackle
looking for lily berries,
looking for blue pearls. Water
holds his eyes. A silver weir.

o

Sand incessantly beckoning. Sandpipers
scurry to erase the loss of their faint
print at the foaming margin.

I

Watch Harry put a toe in.

I

Harry Soot,
unclear, of course, about fire.
        How original, originating,
it really was—
        Forests aflame. Resinous clubs.
In the dark paneled reading room,
a green shade.

        o

        Sand, a cat's cradle fan, and economic.
        Her shave and a haircut, fifteen cents;
        her Oceania nodes of knot
                remembered navigation;
        her numerous fingers interlaced
        with gloves—made of holes—slipped
        successfully over;
                her mediumistic con
        in the dark apparatus, all one, all
        the same nano-rope. This point
        escaped Harry. Harry preferred Ouija
        wavering words, reassured
        by Ouija jerk.

1

Harry is no fool. Harry Soot is shrewd.
Harry has allergies and moods.
Harry lies—he can't
                          help it.
Harry has structure—genes and grammar.
Harry is a detective, but he can't find
    an answer. Harry is violent
and violently quiet;

        01000011

        Sand is sand.

0

Sand insinuated herself. ZaumZoom in,
she has gone ahead. ZoomTzim out,
    she is not behind. To hear,
in her gourd, her mallet-fall, a relation to
    emptiness, finest gauze, so finely
        woven even the strands
                appear to disappear.

        1

        Harry Soot believes he is watching.
        Harry thinks he is in Times Square.
        He is. She is not.

o

Twirly languid blue-eyed blue pearls clearly not Sand.
Down on the fourth harmonic she simply singly for a second
stood, so symmetric, second subsequent swiftly sliding side-
riding slamjamming shivering switching—

  I

  Soot calls it "searching."

o

Sand sings *Nessun dorma* long summer
afternoons in the music room. Heavy red
curtains, gilded chairs, portraits of dead
children. Sand in a window seat
looking out on roses;

  I

  Harry Soot in a seersucker suit
  at the far door, arms
  raised in triumph:
  his play, his score.

o

Sand seeks the scent
              of lemon viburnum,
murmuring purple
of the ringneck doves' soft
gurgle as they walk on the wall
and their syllables spill over and
                   fall
         down a column
         of slowness.
Midnight blue of Krishna's

     I

     shoes. Harry finishes up.

o

Sometimes Sand doesn't come. Fatally
   blocked.
Splurt of sign signage red/blue blood
on the grisly snow. Minutes of arc off.

     I

     Harry swims in adrenalin.

o

Sand might be getting restless.
How does Sand feel about insects
as companions? Does she take
her cue from the alkaloid plants?
What seems to Soot revenge may
seem to her survival. Or
is she incapable of refusal?

I

Soot loves Sand. Every tree,
every wall, a target inscription, pierced
by Tell's weapon. Turn me on,
the swooshing sound Soot hears Sand
murmur.

o

Hold me down, Sand prays, to dusk *&*
musk, purple black sheathed with frost,
the Concord grape of Krishna's shoes
        with golden tips and toes
and soles. The stars are variable sprays,
            golden geometric rays
of twisted silk. Crimson lining unfolding.
Achtung! Loose lips. Beware.

I

Here comes Soot.

o

Sand resounds as long as a whale song
passed along and around the waters
of the world. Like a motherchild pod,
she/they both threatened and succored by
the coasts. Alone in the bay, rolling over and
back beneath the moon, as

        I

        Harry and his cohort heave
        into view, traveling in a pack,
        driving them aground.

o

A housedress of dotted Swiss with a lace
collar. A curling iron, to refresh
marcelled hair. Account books with black,
placeholder ribbons. Linoleum
made to look like a brick floor. Sand
could be retro.

        I

        Soot in tow.

o

Sand's relation to dreams bears
repeating. Was it mentioned?

I

Not necessarily Harry's.

o

As albino cave bats who let go
of coloration, but develop keener
sensors, Sand.

I

Soot, who seeks to catch a falling star
in the monitoring
cave, evolves into colorblind.

1

Harry Soot is that kind of guy. Despite
his lust for lime, despite a savvy sense
of what goes down around such light, Harry
Soot is attached to his memory lines,
crow's feet crinkle, scar arroyos, worry
furrows, wry sag, time written in skin,
in bone, in blood. Chemical peels do not
appeal to him. Nor implant chips (wait until
he gets sick!).

01010011

Sand's unbelievable memory
learned, of course,
not lived.

0

Biocompatible glass?
        Sand looks askance.
Sand an infinite receiver—
infinitely flexible. Beyond
        flex in fact, an infinite
deceiver: Proteus at home.

1

Siren! Circe! screams Soot.

o

Golda called Moshe that Arab.
Golda, schoolteacher, thought
words
          warded off.
Is Golda Sand?

          I

          Is Moshe Soot?
          Is Jerusalem a mass of human names . . .

o

Is Sand (a wafer/chip good as) Gold?

          I

          Is Soot . . . meat?

o

Sand's never the sameness fleeter than
anything Soot could get a hand, a handle,
on. Flickery swift. And yet. One finger
brings her crashing down. Hump Dump.

I

Together again—so fast it made Soot
swoon. An arcade thrill. Cheaper than
medical or bootleg. Purer, too, potent
and hygienic. Claustrophobic—no
establishing shot. Unusually
cold—most color blocked her light.

I

Harry Soot from time to time in the market for swoon.
            Perhaps ever more often. In his dream,
just a year or two ago, he remembered edge, it being
            summoned. People who forget the art
of navigation come to believe the island has sunken;

o

Sand's smile at this juncture, Mona Lisan.

I

Harry Soot's grandmama, Muck Raker Ida Tar . . . .
What a falling off there.

IIIIIIIII

Sand's gramp, grep, Pythagoras.
            She done him proud. It sims.

I

Tangy Soot. Tang-I-Bull Soot.

    o

        Trua-vir Sand. Liv-a-Tru Sand.
        Physics: The Movie. R.I.P.,
        crown assays in a bathtub,
        or Galileo trekking to the far side
        of the valley to touch that blue
        boulder on the ridge.
        And would this prove he saw
        mountains on the moon in any case,
        Sand asks.

    o

Sand, as I said, a marimba player;

    I

        Oozy Soot, Uzi Soot, born to swim,
        born to dance, to paint his face, to lay
        flowers by the dead. Soot will say,
        on any given day, born to fly,
        born to rise—born to escape.

o

Sand's whimsy and scarcity/value? Sand
paints daffodils on the deck of an aircraft
carrier, caps the age of the unknown
                    universe.

    1

    Soot is running out of numbers—not
    populace. Lively virus.

o

If a silly con were all Sand were.

    1

    If an ashy trash were all of Soot.

o

Sand religiously stops. And starts the next thing.

    1

    Bluesy Soot can't conclude.

ABSINTHE 3

PATTI

"What I feel when I'm playing guitar
is completely cold and crazy. It's a test
just to see how far I can relax
into the cold wave of a note.
I never tire
of the solitary E . . . . "

The Red Queen stands on her throne.
Strapped to her head, liquid
crystal numerals
enforce. Or reprieve. What I feel
is completely cold and crazy.
It's a test. I never tire.

ABSINTHE 9

COLETTE

To refuse to choose
or to neglect

to do so: the mother of Colette
turning in her garden, garden of earth

delight: Sido alone by the moon
waiting for a century

plant to bloom cannot spare her daughter.
Not even a moment. Cannot tear,

from the skim and pour of waiting,
rough, edged, time—so

offering
abyss. And Colette took up this

bread which was black
and spat back at Lord Death

the red
pomegranate drops.

ABSINTHE 10

AMMA

In this desert, glass
turns
perfect. All

harshness, raining on it,
grinds away
every jag and nodule;

none of it is blank.
As it ages, it
purples;

even the black
volcanic glass, conchoidal,
sharp, eventually

dissolves
becoming as deep
a pool

as a pupil opening
into
an iris.

ABSINTHE 11

ENORMOUS WASHERWOMEN ON STILTS

This is the Showing to women,
the dream
of being fed. Fed in an attic

in front of a window—
"trees lay bare
. . . in the cold air filled

with sunshine . . . . "
Lifted
from a ditch, Julian of Norwich,

her fourteenth
Revelation found only
in the Long Book.

A window with shutters,
inner and outer, hanging vines
grieving its light.

Fed real bread.

Though it smiled,
the face was grave and slowly
turning, a great gondola flower.

Close your eyes. Shut them. Try.
They are open on both sides.

ABSINTHE 12

DANCER

a spectre, black in the spotlight
on a hub of white cubes
spirals to the floor, sliding bare soles on the floor—

now one with her company, hands braced,
legs flexed, wound like vines or roots drawing
from the ground, molting

dance. None
to remember her thrown off her axis, the arch of her fall
extended, ridden down, perilous

recovery, slowly
cantered
and turned, reversed and turned, reversing and turning . . .

GIBBOUS STATEMENT [+]

    −   entropy

         ()

    +   *decrease* of entropy

         (())

    −   compensated decrease of entropy

         ((()))

    +   *uncompensated* decrease of entropy

            (((())))

    −   impossibility of uncompensated decrease of entropy

         ((((()))))

    +   *reduced impossibility* of uncompensated decrease of entropy

            (((((())))))

                      Im P robability ? 0 − + ??

                −

                  ()
                  +

                           (())

                −

               ((()))
               +

                       (((())))

                −

              ((((()))))
               +

                      (((((())))))   ? 0 − + ??

E.D.: *Tell all the truth, but tell it slant . . .*

[+] Josiah Willard Gibbs (1839–1903), mathematical physicist, although a taciturn man, at one point asks whether there could be a "reduced impossibility of uncompensated decrease of entropy." The phrase made me laugh—the reversing polarities of the concepts, as the string unwound, seemed to cry out for more intuitive expression. Entropy had primarily negative connotations in the 19th century, but in the 20th, as information-measure, shifted polarity *within* itself, bringing another twist to the now-you-see-it, now-you-don't quality of deeply nested statements. I gave Emily Dickinson the last word and in the title term "Gibbous" refer to her, the moon, Gibbs, and those nesting parentheses all at once: "more than half but less than fully illuminated."

X-RAY EYES

If 1 is *unio*
and 2 di-lemma,
if 3 is a witness, or his testimony,
and 4 the quartet, the quire, the square,

who is
5 . . . . . and can I
recognize her by the way she talks
or only by the cones of history

pouring through her, she herself
the X-ray eyes, the Palomar
mirror, central
dissolver who nullifies

size-meaning in one smooth motion
of her telescopic barrel
centered   .
in a truss (the womb was a truss and the arms

of her slight mother, so light
in their touch so definite, swift as quick skies in Northern
summer
clouding and lifting, a soft

                              lilt

and around it, ferocious
self-completing
sentences
exerting control,

                              who

          like a globe-
          or loganberry-flower or fingered hand
          growing out of its wrist

          is formed

          like this (quincunxial
          net, pentagonal,
          ✿

SLIPPINGGLIMPSE

	through a development
	of consciousness I detached myself from
	spontaneous
my mother killed by lightning	expression . . . turned to . . . more
[	systematic
in] a high-risk environment of	electricity water dust and chips
air	that calls for
	special
	breathing
	apparatus
vision	hearing protection
	body
	armor . . . insulation . . . I
	undo by violence air
	hammers
	carbide cutters diamond corers saws
	hydraulic rams gantry cranes
millions of years	of geologic material-forming processes
each stone I carve . . . [I] convolve	
with mathematical ideas . . . the form	
that no one	
has ever felt	walked around or
	crawled through

rules calculate
and generate the work
Bense and Barbaud changed my thinking

for each Laserglyph a random selection

4

—from this repertoire of 23,040
diagonal-paths
in a 6-d hypercube—

flattened into visibility :
a 2-d sign of great spatial ambiguity

animation
hangs onscreen

bring light
into the body and hold it
there

I have one now
one billion years old
waiting

toward a rational construction

day after day
a different image
appears

seeing is forgetting the name
of what you see

very slow-motion
flicker

figurine tokens to stylized text :
the *evolution* of notation . . .
turning . . .
back

I learn my form my (subtractive) form

from computed information

like learning a piece of
music by heart or a choreographic
sequence

    treading a wave

the heaviest-duty black industrial
enamel I could find
    toxic colloidal gunk
broken up with red wine
India ink
sludge from the bottom of the brush jar

created this very lyrical and delicate

image landscape on the surface
a performance so convincing people
swear

it is photography

so it was self-organizing?

totally
    well

I finally learned to see
beyond the retinal
    experience

eighty-five percent—
    which I liked

a scanner starts at the beginning
and moves ever so slowly
to the end of the scan
it may take 30 seconds or so

this is just what the Quick-TimeVR
movies do but on a horizontal plane

you | join

the ends so you just turn centered
in an infinite image loop
onscreen

somebody will shoot all the backgrounds
somebody will shoot all the people

all the people on blue-screen   tribal   *mask*   zone

somebody will shoot all the clouds   historical   *mirror*   zone
you're going to replace into the sky
                                        numerical   *image*   zone

the compositor composits it all

output to
whatever format you want
video DV film whatever

Quick-Time Virtual Reality

to break down or bring out
the scanner pieces   like turning an urn
photographing all sides

so they become an event
use a cursor to travel around it or you can
be   inside
take your pick

QTVR space
scanner space

the original panorama has a very quiet

quality about it because the beginning
and the end
join seamlessly

I work   inside
"the urn"
it seems like reality to me

flesh
format

physical   presence   luminosity
wanting to touch

please don't touch
almost any
             photographic paper will
fingerprint if you touch

huge failure rate
which I now take for granted
         I can work
with some accident
but I still have a great many disasters
usually through pushing something
too far

        the air   lives

by turning green
not struck from stones
not blossoming out of twigs
        within the wind a little wind
          within the light a greater light
not rooted
in a power to beget
        Ignota Lingua
        H. of B.

greenness not a color

complication of the process

longwinded
enumeration

flax to linen rag to paper

Graces flying from the Hunter
pass the woman weeding flax

who detains him

whiling away the fatal hour

with the tedious story

distracting aggressor
ghosts all night until the cock crew

thrown in the ditch
pulled out by the hair
skinned heckled broken scorched
washed in lyes worried

to pulp

as flax is hackled with a comb of thorns
grapes are ripped from stalks
with the comb of the fingers

I have not tortured
the plants
nor have I shoveled them into the oven

buried blue-eyed flowering plucked root
& branch retted soaked to partial rotting
scorched over fire bound battered dressed
rippled with hackle combs and thorns
drawn fiber spun thread woven *linen*
bleached on grass pierced needles sewn
shirt worn to rag rent drowned calendered
    dried to paper   written on

It is another who did this
and brought them to me

I ate innocently

spoken to the loaf

[goddess]
    Reply seized [the divine son] Death

                    to cut
         winnow roast and scatter   for birds to eat to break the spell
                             scattered not sown   older
                             than bread

                             a feast "Denial"
                             in the month Denial
               rent to pieces   at which all dogs
               by "dogs"   met in the market are killed
               harvesters
               masquerade

    passion of the flax   to seem to refer not to divinized
                         barley of Babylonia
                            nor sacred green ear of Eleusis
                               but the child born

                          House of Bread Beth-Lehem

seven virgin disciples
    whose flesh shines during torture
as white as the shining

               silvery

                           fiber of the flax

              silver

                         grain

photochemicals flood the emulsion
acidic and basic waves compete on film
     to fix
            or strip suspended
          silver

       palette of stained glass
              childhood
       window
light as it falls is winnowed plucked
     by the Polaroid

image that records pure saturated light

what language do you write in

C++

do you work in the Mac or PC world

the SGI world
which is doing so poorly
Unix and SGI are my loves

   I have also been making photograms
     the paper negatives are striking
   in their rich luxurious warm blacks

I teach compositing and effects
using Flame
and Flint
applications by Discrete Logic

you've got purists to whom
algorithmic art
is the only way to go
but then who's to say that's right

I find myself kind of alone at the Academy
they're into turning out people
who can get jobs
in the animation industry

                    Genetic Brushes
an evolutionary model where you could
         breed two brushes together
they would make a whole new brush

brush over the entire image algorithmically
no human
intervention other than
the basic parameters

                    brush size color angle etc.
          calculated
based on info from the image
                    whether it was luminance
                         or hue   or . . .

                    Denial
          a bed of slender
          reeds

living on light

               (. . . to come

                              at the bottom of the food chain
underwater

numerical   *image*   zone

(. . . to come

                              (. . . to come

                    of slipping glimpse

          a realm

VERSUS VEGA : PRECESSING

That first fact that a Star
Appears fixed, a *Nail*
Of the North, a Sky
Hole to hold Earth axle—
Spin-steer, Lodestar

Cynosura.

Pole Star to the Akkadai,
Spinning Girl,
Girl with a Shuttle in China.
Vega in Lyra—tortoise shell—
Solar System flying toward her.

13 millennia on,

Once again Vega Pole Star—
Will on Earth any (be to) see her?
13 millennia back, bards, bull-
Jumpers, cats, the new
Great Lakes, blue-eyed flax.

DRAGON LOGIC

. . . there are songs to sing beyond / the human

—PAUL CELAN

Breathturn

Why do the poets of the present not speak of it?

—RICHARD P. FEYNMAN

Lectures on Physics

THE RADIO hope
        access to the dead
        access to the lightfuzz that lived
            in crystal sets slipping feet tripping
            wings in vacuum tube towers
            in the Hendrix amplifier
            from the back
            cities of snubnose glass open to view
in old radios was the RCA
        dog fooled
        as fully as I was *people*
in the radio all I meant
by people in the radio too delicate too breakable
            for my harsh moves
            too wrapped in an upswept case
                with a dial face
                intermittent as clouds
                static
                music
            too apt to erupt or be unplugged
            too innerly unreachable
            by my clumsy moth

AND of course it is
a wave a sound broken into bits
threaded through numbers

you will take me to mean
nautiline spirals
Florentine chapels Doric temples
al-Hambran Taj Mahalian
symmetries Persian figures

or will you understand it as
the undecidability
between code and capital
the immaterial bio-economy
essence of bio-information
packaged in crystal hint of jasmine

no you are a fancier of stars
you think Arecibo mega array
the billionsfold
data re-splayed quintillionfold

or eyes forward you mention
video macro attractors CNN
blog minis all pull all
seduction neural icon
image flux the real

RARA AVIS

telepresence installation by Eduardo Kac

not the old vicarial
        Holy Communion
nor the older
        surgery
        pregnancy
        sex
instead
        another newer way to enter each other to share
        the same
        (telematic) co-ordinates
to share
        via circuitry and hardware (these
        vary) surveillance an ambience physical robots and avatars
wander
the augmented body invaded hosts
        ping body
        composite unfragmented neither
        all-here not all-there sliding in
        shifts
the viewer is transported into the aviary
        and sees from the pov of the *Macowl* a telerobotic tropical
        (eyes front so owl) macaw (CCD camera eyes)
Voilà! space instanter Virtual
        connected through the Net
        as well remote
participants share owl's body
        vicarially in and out of the macaw
        other birds in the aviary (flying) 'real'
            though for them too this is negotiated

locals :: remotes animals :: telerobots
for sale
        freeware gets a grayscale
        commercial product color
        color feed to multicast frame rates available to still fewer
profession older than the oldest
vicarial lure vampiric pull past skin body in body

ALGORITHM

Recipe

Ingredients   *Instructions*

instructions   map a metaphor or more
                                 to computational processes (not
                                         to *compositional*
                                                         capiche?)

                                 twiddle (de dee) tweak (de dum)
                                 execute / run   repeat
                                 till well (enough)

                                 done oh
                                 will this one
                                 halt

MEASURABLE pleasures
30 seconds or so of a non-changing environment
are enough to relax *Octofungi*

inorganic anemone
electro-sensitive to light
whose small arms tip and reach extend and rock

a plug-in neural net—
its ingredients *mass : atoms*   whereas
bit packet life

can transit the solar system in hours its ingredients *instructions*—
(only who to receive?
what storage-and-expression system?)

Whale ancestor coming ashore air-breather mammal
after an eon returned to the ocean—

Digital biotics well-adapted to space : is this life
going *back* or   moving *on*   escaping
earth and the coils of DNA as the algorist asserts—

Cross it! Jump the *bit*omic / *atom*ic barrier declared frontier
the airy cages hacked
reconfigured   felled   unspared—   are we clear?

THE SAME interaction the same charge and enormous

speed my brother Finn my virtual my transient

twin seething with energy some

or none or any at all

except that one

number that makes me

real and not

him he the ghostly the free

loader the thief exuberant slid in under the bell

33 SYMMETRY AXES X 40 ORTHOGONAL TRIPLES; OR, FREE WILL, REVISITED

Are you kidding? Quarks, too, can *choose*?
      Conway and Kochen, old dragons, well
vetted, claim—no—prove, if given a free hand to choose

        their gear direction while quizzing quarks with questions,
          taking their measure, then, too, whim-

driven *&* not determined, a particle's response. To be
      precise—*the universe's response near* the particle un-
determined by the Whole prior history of World Time *&* Space.

        In fairness, it's the theory's "strong"
          (min, spin, twin) form—could they claim more?

Imagine haranguing electrons,
    just say no—
Imagine addressing zoomers *sans* apparatus. Up and at it,

        again, are you, pairs of them grumble, maybe even hiss;
          gauging us, too, in their stinging way.

IN that shot they take

        on the water at night from a rowboat
        moored somewhat south of dead center
            light from the moon is older
      than light from the trees
                  light from the lapping
      shore's grassy wash older than light
      from the fish-jump near their oar
            pulled
      back on board

a tissue of histories   no snapped shut

      moment though light hit lens in an instant
          (deferring all stories of where a photon
      goes) for the sake of survival
            for the sake of passage ease
      the sake of cosmic reading
      ease ease in
         to this none
           can
      exist, *compañera*, feel it know no instantaneous

photo   'the whole'   lake

WATER, WATER EVERYWHERE

WILLIAM KATAVALOS
interviewed by DEBORAH GANS
Bomb 97 FALL 2006

Katavalos—architect whose work I crave—
claims he came to love liquidity via language :
"piss, shit, snot, scum, bile, and puke . . . . "

Why crap and jism, crud, seep, fail this list
derived from Joyce I can't imagine,
not to mention blood. What he craves, amniotic

incorporation, tunnels, not towers;
hates the surface of the sea, won't swim,
only dive in a bubble-less re-breather.

He requires separation of mass from surface,
mass liquid, surface sheets of plastic,
creating ballooned mesodermal organs

within the body house—skeleton and skin
identifiable, still, but so subordinate so shifting
he jokes "form swallows function," and exults

"the transparency of a mass like water
is like having liquid concrete."
Architect whose work I fear—here, a Mafioso feel.

I do agree, I want more than a box with a door
on it, or a minimized surface; although
so many would be glad for it, content to lose

rooms within rooms onto rooms "you can go
through via apertures, in almost . . . peristaltic
progress" (department stores I can't get out of!)

or Italian towns, or Tiffany's mansion now
burned down, "a hundred rooms and every [one]
a different organic form." The secret charm,

sudden Hide-and-Seek : lost "[i]n this place
you would wear waterproof
clothing . . . wearable computers, e-broidery . . . . "

He focuses on "*inner* body . . . including the kidneys
. . . the ureters . . . bringing the outside in, it is
the inside, inside out," which, to my mind, undoes

'inner', another non-transformative flip;
yet conduits, "hydroforms—hydrocolumns,
hydroarches, hydrovaults," on paper as seductive

as what he was seduced by, Palladian villas, vacuum
domes, and a quality of light like Lalique, ornamental
complexity, the Sansovino library in Venice,

Debussy's Engulfed Cathedral, a "Breton
legend . . . the Cathedral of Ys sinks into the sea each day
at sunset, rising again at sunrise with great majesty . . . . "

Pisces without Fire Signs, spacey, I neglect
gravitational grounding, but the air
in motion, the wind tells me the Cathedral of

Is sinks into the sea still shimmering at sunset
maintaining ghost presence, breathing all through
the night (default surveyor stars marking out

sea surface, sometimes storming auroral)
before rising again with the sun, with a majesty I
bring, I accord, awed—but also without me.

"Is Security the Next Aesthetic in Architecture?"
He means not living "in a black box with a bunch
of black boxes, living blind." He means

a house you understand where you can
—yourself—generate power, know how
things are grown (hydroponic), how to fix it;

"architecture of mass that does not have to be
quarried or carried to the site," degrees
of transparency easily changed.

He claims kinship to "The Glass Chain. The crystal
house becomes the liquid house," he says,
and says light penetrating stained

glass without puncture instructs on virgin
birth. He is asserting muliebrity. He's right about
calling on mathematics, "like using a ten-ton press

to crack a walnut," but has become obsessed
with Feynman's obsession, 243; his own,
761; and 100.115.965.22, the anomalous

magnetic moment of the electron, most thoroughly
verified, carefully measured in the history
of physics— He engages blocks of numbers,

begins to predict numeric masses flushing from
accelerators : "it's sub-numeral : good for nothing
but describing nature." "It is organic. It is . . . numeric

animation." "Architecture . . . a succession
of gender geometries." He is
a professor : "[the] temple mount was used for

sacrificial surgery." "[A]rchitecturalized"
as "geometric dentils[,]"
" . . . blood dripping over its edges . . . . "

∞ INFINITE ways to change continuously lapping licking staying
at (near) equilibrium

7 but   seven stable ways to change abruptly   *jump*
Hell's kitchen smoke plume fire cat
something's got to give it *duh*
does . . . spectacular
collapse
            . . . or the baby's nap . . . unfolding

stably disappearing stability a
ha downdraft snowflake oh also snow
ball rolling into mind soot chippiness ice

utter irrelevance
            scale | laws | causes | radiation
to the form to
                        the gliding shape the wind the word the (class 4)
computation

KEEP it | kill it   *call it!*   up

or down ↓ data warrant data thumb data agency security arts
department *dependency* danger-wrangler in the pit
handicapping on the fly data are not
                      evidence
          for that to which they *drownage* attest

       the horse dissolved into monkeys

and the quiet into comatose lady at the mirror
bar late afternoon truthfully there is no noon in the timeless
      old hotel cool concentric waves of dulled semicircle silver open
          sparks shower from the live cage monkeys
gingerly testing fences in the urban forest

       every junction is a number a corner a vertex

every junction a tone   intervals   swimmingly overlap confines within
      the octave Octavia swallowing mandorla martini
                glasses of unclouded
gin in the permadim grotto
of echoing surfaces a faint jade in the beveled edge hint of mint

COMELY SUBSTITUTIONS

Gibbs gifted Maxwell with a plaster cast
the size of a fist. Locked in its grip

each & every history of water; the cast, a grandsire
node on the traceroute of legible images of total time.

Talan made a movie, nipple tree of Nowhere, *Ingenstans*,
Sweden's riverbank where the children drowned,

children run over by a boat—by a bot. Why seek
to tell them apart (children and *bots*) reliably

or fast? To keep polls (clicks) unpolluted, discount
ersatz million hits. People suck at this, too slow,

run over; so, yes, an automatic application : you play,
it gets smarter. Talan cites Duchamp, *Network of Stoppages*.

•

Cortical CPU network body—angled upon it, slices
and shadows, assembled, loom by torchlight; comely

substitutions, cool, as-if-new, code-views expose-
distort, as they blow up, manifolded-ness-entanglement.

Jeremy's, volumetric; Talan urges tesseractic. No more!
Reverse-engineering 'nature'? Nature, please, is Disney—

Reverse instead reverse-engineering's computational
feat—or drive it forward, for we tire, conscious

choice, of the sea on fire—we cannot chance
that the oil would stop without it, without *simulation*.

The deep water drilling didn't *start* without one.
Apocalypse, how long? Eleven-million years or so

ago, sonar probes, ping-echoing easy-pass dolphin bands
began to sentinel-haunt, to test, to re-shape the coasts.

VARIETIES of ecocide : does it matter
text 30001

viral vs. nuclear warheads :
answers at 10

we hear from gamers math professor
simulators those in actual rehearsal

involuntary
immersion in the real : a pharmal

target each blockbuster drug
to reach each until

it goes off-patent
factoid : leeches make shocking comeback

TWO dragons
keep a pearl
            in the air untouched
if yes then no if no then yes

untouchable between them
sustained between them
                        perhaps
the flow of air

each guarded by nine more
rampant
            ready
should one falter perhaps

at long
            last
able to
withdraw untouched

into stones to function there
mapped by slow
domain
if no then yes if yes then no

EVERYONE knows that dragons don't exist. But
while this simplistic formulation may satisfy
the layman, it does not suffice for the scientific
mind . . . .

Cerebron, attacking the problem analytically,
discovered three distinct kinds of dragon :
the mythical, the chimerical, and the purely
hypothetical. They were all, one might say,
nonexistent, but each nonexisted in an entirely
different way . . . .

Suppose, for example, one organizes a hunt for
such a dragon, surrounds it, closes in, beating
the brush. The circle of sportsmen, their weapons
cocked and ready, finds only a burned patch of
earth and an unmistakable smell :
the dragon, seeing itself cornered, has slipped
from real to configurational space.

—Stanislaw Lem, *The Cyberiad*

so it comes in the fullness of mind and it came to
pass to collapse the column *columns begone*
a central sanctum cleared covered by a dome
well first one arch two then a few intersecting
high heavenly span if the dome were inverted
should it become some huge dish
what pulls it together would pull it apart
if it could be placed in orbit it would drift apart
a chain is used around the dome of St. Peter's in Rome

a chain is used around the dome of St. Peter's in Rome
if it could be placed in orbit it would drift apart
what pulls it together would pull it apart
should it become some huge dish
high heavenly span if the dome were inverted
well first one arch two then a few intersecting
a central sanctum cleared covered by a dome
pass to collapse the column *columns begone*
so it comes in the fullness of mind and it came to

GROTHENDIECK

sees everything globally from the beginning Hironaka
        said *no coordinates no*
  *equation*s

roller coasters have no sudden on
    a dime
change of direction however steep
      no cusp
      no crossing through themselves—

    their shadows do : sharp projections of the smooth

pulling back
    to the smooth
from tangle   local
      tumult disappears : only *global*   lift
left

inside the crush cross point so multifarious—a many nenny
whorled

    blow   it up (gentle difficult
balloon work) make it
     smooth

LINES spears nets knots have-knots

                                         no-horse

they are not here

                          they are straddling sand sky peer wait
for wind
          shift manhigh water python tunnel to span
swallow mansea creature ocean deepest pounding breath
                      sea surface scumble sullen south
wind bitter flat as for with Easter
                              Island they wait forward

they are not here with us thus we see we are
not here the smallness
                    of us
refugee camp concert audience collapsed
towers no prior us constituted thus
                            seconds in seconds

dream of we
          a garden's worth of marigold bluebell creatures in the lily
trumpets tubes
                        radio cities

Duke a hundred years ago stood up on the "bluebird" the cataclysmic
wave the spawn the lethal avalanche
                   from Diamond Head to the Harbor
1.75 miles my

back in collapse not a duke not a sleek invention not a
kayak not a wave
flotsam kelpish
alignment alone thrust position on the wall averts wipeout

the tatting aunt bore to her grave for want
of a human relay
vital connection correct protocol
transmission fear of dissipation dissolution drizzle lethal
error
wordhoard treasure   here be dragons rather
die
a wooden barb may be parried but a verbal barb cannot
he tao rakau e taea te karo, he tao kupu e kore e taea te karo

using a fishhook made from the jawbone
of her grandmother no-horse

AS MUCH contingency as craft
Longyearbyen Doomsday Ark
seed vault on Svalbard

going *on* is the enormous
thing I do Agnes not
forward first an eschewed

then an indefinable now almost
inexistent direction but
dimensions abound we stipulate

three (it feels small) million
seeds Agnes in the desert
Martin mostly alone said

BURNING BRIAR SCANNING TUNNEL

there is a zombie at the wheel
who finds acceptable all risk

(his flesh looks like mine)

a crinkle monkey in the swamp
mind tricky and brisk

(his moves feel like mine)

headless mannequin draped
white print snakeskin dress

(pale fakery filling me with dread)

a boneless man used up
by apparatchik juggernaut

(scrivener like me)

the one who hoped to poach
cockroach strategy adrift

(like me time-amnesic overreaching)

cord-cut all   beyond the call
to heal or heel   *fold   molt*

(wormhole crush crash course)

UNSOLVED PROBLEMS

chance has no memory
so we choose
sealed by amnesia
to undergo the formality of occurring

mysteries bear
in mind have no relation—thus
any linkage—whatsoever
to unsolved problems

in a world divided
into what *can* be divided
without
damage (magnitudes metrics . . .)

what cannot?
what if divided changes its nature?
duration distance solitude
life-

time *obedience* : not ten-hut
military
rather *ob-au-di-re* (hear . . . thoroughly)
then too   endurance

you already know what to do

I sigh untense my feet
I am grateful to the universe for
this reprieve

says the cult narrative

I freeze I see I am
its secret admirer
Armageddon clean slate

restive tugging at
its halter how
instantly

it hits—

fleeting
as ripples flowing off the rim of a clam's
fleshy foot body probingly slowly extending onto shifting

sand I

in the unclear
quiet
wait

V : WAVETERCETS / LOSING L'UNA

26

When Columba converted the mermaid,
which of them said,
"Is it really

27

you?"
And then, after a time, who
replied, "How good is God's memory?"

28

Struggling to ward off being mounted,
since this would leave the chorus
without a conductor, and sensing a near-

29

lag in the beat, the man with too much state
in his head holds tempo,
pacing, tone, and volume constant,

30

but instructs the drummer (who is rarely, really
never, mounted) to vary
the breaks, to force possession

31

or reprieve it, techniques
to project
from psyche to physique

32

to psyche. A waltz
frames the mind of coquetry;
a tango, desolation.

33

That drummer in control during ritual
—but not of it;
that drummer in control during ceremony,

34

barely of it, has changed his name.
He plays Intendo on the virtual
causeway to the titular

35

see: he is a mystery fan.
Is it really you,
he longs to say, but I swim away,

36

repeating his beat, his cadence,
with my tail,
so opening a channel.

37

A channel only open, not a code, no
message, for him
to break. I fall away

38

from his design and say
to myself, so, we must meet apart
in a time

39

of no tomorrow, no pleading, no art,
time of waiting, a miracle mer-main
of hallucinated hearing.

40

Fin(-ger) to finger, I shiver,
am calm: the reef embraces the water
that wears it

41

down.
You have seen, with your own eyes, yes?
Or believed the lie that it can't

42

be lost, that it lives
somewhere else, somewhere safe
as it is not

43

in that slippery, silken twist
of cord
run by rhythm through psyche

44

to physique to sea to sky to water falling, dripping
with the sound of the water bird veering
on whose back

45

the earth rides.
Apprehended where every cell engaged: an entire body,
paralyzed, knees

46

drawn up, nails drawing blood,
neck rigid, tears streaming from shut
eyes, locked jaw, grinding teeth:

47

that silent song
possesses every
Erzulie, Her every *serviteur,* whose fragile

48

beauty, whose zephyr lilting lightness
has been tempered
by the cracking whip, by Petro fire,

49

Erzulie Ge-Rouge, who comes to the poor
in pink and white perfection, cologne
lavished from a faceted bottle and a swath of lace

50

down the skirt of her improvised dressing table,
she is almost Tennessee's
Blanche, whispering coquette, all

51

roses, shells, and smile,
until she starts to weep.
And cannot

52

be stopped, every cell engaged.
Is Tuesday her day? Rose her scent?
Titon

53

will tell you, you must feast her.
You must replenish
Source, would you keep her,

54

going back and forth not as a footpath
but a smile.
Not as a footpath, as a meal.

55

We do not eat to turn into food—food which we think
we can reach out and take,
but we cannot take what can only be given.

141

The Occitanian world, a resisting tide, a river
of peoples in the honey-
combed caves near Toulouse, near Marseilles.

142

As electrons rush the tube
at one-fifth the speed of light, do they testify
to a prehistoric rupture,

143

a Glacial flood, or the dangerously close-coming
passage of the moon as Roadrunner boulders, meteorites
careen through the sky, crater the earth,

144

or was an inner sense of hearing-counting lost
when the children stopped coming together
in a brood, in the easy spring, conceived at Midsummer

145

and began to be born *throughout* the year, whenever.
And began to be garnered as workers
in a settling world. Their,

146

now unpredictable, mothers
no longer wander.
Someone has seen—

147

Who but I, says the bird.
And it flies away.
Renewal

148

assumed
to the ranking ladder and ranked below power,
ownership, fixed place, Force, to enforce.

149

"Pure gold, not alchemist's gold . . . but the true metal
dug out from mines where dragons stand watch."
Viète Isagoge, 1591. "He is referring,"

150

says André Weil, Simone's
brother, "to the power and scope of the new algebra.
The ore is from Diophantus."

156

A plaintive tone, as in
"Procne is among the slaves," that embroidered text
of a woman raped and her tongue cut out

157

by her brother-in-law. She is trying to address
her sister. And does. And they serve him
his child for dinner. And turn into birds.

158

Blank birds, they blend—into one name, Philomel.
Medieval story of the nightingale,
pressing her breast onto thorns, who can't remember

159

why she mourns. A real witch doesn't cry,
a real witch can't float.
Weight her down, if she drowns, you were correct

160

in your suspicions. Someone,
somewhere, saw, once, for the first time,
a rape, but which of them knew it?

170

How to make nothing of something.
Don't take me amiss. I mean nothing
by it, I mean only lightness,

171

a zephyr, a lilt, evanescent
yielding,
I mean electronic.

172

The ore is from Diophantus.
"The idea is to form the algebra of sections
of the bundle over the leaf space.

173

[Gap] . . . closed currents
on the space of leaves . . . a new technique— . . . to . . . reach
below the Planck scale and attempt to decipher

174

the fine structure
of space-time." *Notices of the AMS,* August
1997.

206

If we understood red, her web
blocking the path, glistening in sun, as the strong
door to dust, as a form

207

of strong transparence,
protecting the chalice, the bear, the canting horn,
filigreed, veined with dark.

208

Fear in the nursery.
Uninvited guest.
A spindle gift.

209

A child sleeps for a hundred years
behind the briar hedge.
One prick of blood.

210

What does matter about the function
is the nature of the peak
at its very center. Green and graceful witch . . .

216

. . . tracery of frost on glass.
Any
section of such blown up—equally

217

exquisite, detailed, ever, over and over, a never
ending,
never decaying, never

218

exactly
the same pattern—recognizable at once.
Begin with a closed interval, include ends,

219

take out the middle: on the separated them, do
again, again . . . creating, or leaving, a structure more and more
open, of sparkling points.

220

Indra's Net? Cantor dust.
Do there exist beings where all take each other
into account, in their very core?

221

The smallest particles.
Renormalized photons.
List. I say *list,* that long implicit, blurred string

222

my mother
left me.
Isomorphism, another name for coding.

223

Words of others.
Lists and strings are fluid data structures.
The Glacier calving, enormous roar

224

into a gray silent sea,
turquoise
lining.

225

Krill stains the snow
and the breasts of the penguins.
1/10th of a second,

226

the time it takes
to recognize your mother.
From one hundred million

227

retinal dots
to one
word

228

—*is it really*
you
I long to say?

229

Skim and teeter
of a moving balance, her beret,
Simone's,

230

as she stands
at prayer, very
slightly

231

swaying—swaying in the air
above her
an emerald darner

232

hovers;
that, I think, she hears, but
does not see.

NEW POEMS

THE BODY OBSOLETE

FOR KAFKA

subtly the praying mantis lifts
its leaf-stick body laced with fire glint
—engraved tracing of dioxin

a condensery become a crematory
—mint— was that
what was meant?

"a book" succumbs
the sea frozen fathoms thick
axe handle porous—riddled—blight

BODY OF TWISTED TANGLED SURFACES

                  beyond connectivity
beyond skeletal   interim
bendable
                  body
                       body heap

proper harnesses and edges
           molded stapled suctioned
           no

rupture restively re-captured   X-
                  plodes in
          side the
                     / mine

C.T. OR H.

Cyberterror, as we say C.T.
or H. for hacktivism—NSA?
Does it, or DHS, attack itself
to leverage public funding, i.e. raid

or ride our Coffer sorely rid by debt
in red/blue garb? A disappearing Cloak
of Digitality set to reroute
our men of stealth into our men of steal—

O brave new Traceless-as-Transparency! O
Warriors high on Nyah-Nyah—you can't see!

INVISIBLE, VISION

explodes!
   a clover of stagings

      1st leaf (Plato
      &) the prize-pox of potential
      paradox

2nd leaf a ladder of logical
      types   3rd orthogonal
   (Bateson—or Bertie)   dimensions (Gibbs as many
                              as you like) more than you can think

               4th stages stratigraphy
                     geology "levels" (Darwinian)
                           plateaux

      5th a juggling jester
            (wysiwyg Bird's Nest calli-
      graphi-
            cally scaling) gestures
            forth

COLLINS SAYS HOW

clock   -wise   leading-to-trailing-
edge it grows   shifts   twists halfway up
        side on   to side other—

maximal   rich surface of coherent curvature   negative
    curvature   throughout
Astrolily   midline crest and trough   trace helices

        —elegant   as   it may be
little pleasure in   making
      blossom portion faceted   un-

dulating succession of planes   phased so when
           S's   intersect
line of intersection nails   helical path

    delving into details   template conversion
rotation-aware   hand-carved
      calculation

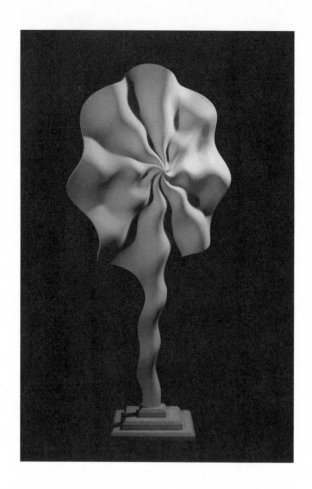

3.03.15 EMAIL FROM COLLINS . . . IMAGES OF ASTROLILY (COULD BE VIEWED

AS A SPACE-CREATING deployment pattern . . . of unimaginably energized quantum
flux trillions of a nanosecond after the detonation of an inherently unstable singularity,
the condition of a multiverse I presume in which other universe might emerge with
parameters consistent with the evolution of consciousness, perhaps sometimes ones
in which sentience is less susceptibility to fear and suffering as dynamics conferring
reproductive advantage and therefore with planetary theaters more comfortable to a
humanely empathetic moral compass than our own . . . brent

—BRENT COLLINS, SCULPTOR

GORMLEY VS. STELARC

STELARC *Parasite: Event for Invaded and Involuntary Body*

          seed pod inner bomb

                suture shock
                wired up convulsive gridflesh
                cringe connect

           or platoon squared off

yards apart
separated men cast from iron anchored deep
naked cool as Greeks wade into the sea the sea
       ascends
over
them and sloshingly retreats original
       alone
fixed staring staring out

orphan seizes breath dancer step stalker game woman
       climbing
birth mountain her pain   "Becom[e] exotic"

unrecognized face   face in the well
       face plugged in the wall

GORMLEY *Another Place*

INTRODUCTIONS

1

I live in a splendid city
Capital of capital ruinful ruinous ruin us Noo Yawk
Plastered painted dripping with myopic
Gold at dawn
Rivers of tall glass gold even with my glasses on
Green carbon footprint an imperial minim
Sky spectrum at sunset ravishing toxin induced
Blue fumous purple

2

I am as alone as survival permits
Not at all and quite a bit
Only my afflicted daughter more so
Hidden in a land of flaunted wealth
Organ rebellion no site safe
Neural paroxysms gag on water
Choke on air
Bio-integrity fails to adapt
Extended care

3

Fay folk wee sprites inside
Lily of the valley cordon by the garage
On the way to the back alley
Beneath the raised screen porch
Stopping the jalopy with built-up pedals
To discover garnets grenadine black currant eyes in a twirl

Upon twirl of lace Queen Anne's in a meadow O
Of course not a meadow
Some back lot some abandoned weed field
No one liked it then but she and me
The aimless caravanning
Elvishness still alive

I CHOOSING BY CHANCE

man with two dongs splayed on the bed entire
sheets of Chinese red Turkey red stamps stamped with gold
calligraphic patterns I peel turn out to be

the wrong denomination why had the woman sold me
that—people are waiting—never make it out to party
on the patio alone stepping down to a grotto

underground flooded iceberg underbelly turquoise
blue tentacled dark I can't tell I can't sort
the arrangement of waters I can see into a cave

back-lit frosts of pale breath rise from alabaster bowls
recessed in the walls on the walkway damp slightly afraid
not exactly of drowning some breathless gap

closing but predominant refreshment
ease—only me still—any—here—I'm only one there
a mailing that can't or hasn't taken place

2 SHAPE SHIFTING

simulation turns logical
then to temporal then then

she dies runaway regeneration self-corrective *calm* or
oscillation is the Cretan lying yes / no / yes / no / until

the ink
dries a cartridge emptied all

shards and bits rend
or render flesh a child said *what is*

the grass pressing
the glass

3 RANDOM WORLDS

creation hymns sung sing forth creation
solitary packwolf   chitin wing   intensive transformation

jars of night unboundedness burst through

suddenly empty everything slows to
through a riveting whirlpool

ear awoken to the sound of blood coursing
unable again to track anything but that

4 CLASPING THE TRACKLESS

never a trace
no mark
sweet slot so unlike
any spot on a curve

radical unobservability
complex quantities
infinite matrices *every*
path taken

no configuration
dis-articulation
if it happens
to arrive a calling card

scanned spectral slice
disassembled disjecta
Venetian-blinding matter
all phenomena

with new mathematical
operators applets
a hard class way to speak
about the massless

5 THE POUR THE PORE

tonight

deep red bands of trim
the chalet drips paint
unshipshape chalet

today

snow erosion of the roof
lichen and storks on the roof
condensate of holes the roof

I LIVING WITH CONSEQUENCES

neither the sand diviner nor the makeover undercover virtuoso's therapeutic necessarily
much less auspicious *what auspices at Aulis* Iphigenia's caustic murder team deciding
what to descry

nor spontaneous shift to Asperger expertise mindmeld with 'machine' information that
exceeds unaugmented human was there ever any other kind I wonder are we near to now
or farther from

lumbering bear life roaming ocean life attacked back in the day a recognized cry—
neither flight nor all this light has brought us closer to the sky

2 HEAD *&* WALL

soggy crystals of honey stitch my donkey head donkey master still drubbing

3 LIVING WITH EQUATIONS, RIEMANN

choric continuum of patches

"I do think that a solution will eventually be found. I don't think it is a result which is unprovable. Maybe though the proof will be so involved that the human brain will not catch up with it." —ATLE SELBERG

WHATEVER—

used to work in wood not anymore
sinter laser in its bath of dust

a Bodleian of deep sea ocean cores
crashes Cloud-kept gated by some volt-

age vaulting over servers ridge to ridge
reckless bridgeless ropeless headlong leap

accomplished no bravado only *zest*
elderness extends antennal trees

and very . . . very . . . slowed dock of the bay
stutters ghosts abortuses extinctions

Python Perl Ruby Lisp Titanium
kludging glitch attendants 'make my day'

point pixel privilege   Analog in D
embedded-*not*   it's Digital iN A

cached everywhere I execute/play/pay
trump geophysics with G-locatives

send ribbon worms extruding into space
tubers to digest text into skin

snarls of code are catching in my throat
Gorilla Glass re-mazing my attention

while the floating turquoise berg is sensing
a universe all hum: start tuning in

whistlers on the line cross hemispheres
a-biotic lives are hard some rust some shine

on Gargle Earth's white cube black box
light strings matter-forth—as Columbines

suppose stability flatlines our brains
not that we're wrong but what if we are real

caru   O.E.   care   sorrow   grief
ocean ice-sheet SPF 1 million

ribbons barrel along not their cross-sections
reclaim as neo-pagan witches say

difference or degree a sack of nodes
at odds irreconciled unconsoled

their cry for justice *founded* such that each
planetarian be held each sleep

corral from silence its own vibrant tone
Precambrian *Heimweh* yes 2000 Ma

[*Ma* means now a Million-years-*ago*]
past snowball earth past muck if stopless flood

be Grail be gusher geyser-forcing Goal
the ultimo of any univers-

al urge it's yet no ultimate of mine
I change the locks I choose an ancient sea

its uncaused stasis/strew one salt-filled chance
to pledge to pr-e-quals their lost jubilee

to say we know this needs to be redone
remade rethought redeemed re-hoped rerun

ANOTHER "QUESTION CONCERNING TECHNOLOGY"

I

teeth bared   barring the male
      precisions of jaw   raw   speech
                      intent
        cave lioness patrolling the pool
          cradle boat   sealed with pitch

2

vulture-bone   mammoth-ivory bits   *1000 and more*   re-
     assembled by Marie   *5*   pentatonic
      holes   *35-*
1000 years   cave concert hall years a   *V-*

     shaped   mouth-

piece pitches lo-pitched blows across a wide range of cave
bear femur-flute tones   mute-swan bone
    flute   patient   technician
     43000 years   unaccompanied

                 toc

3

    then Bach   who walked 200 miles
to hear an organist
     &
back

4

carved in ivory mammoth-tusk
carved string-net hood

last night (5/6) she came
stepped forward slightly built
woman African hair short
grizzled bent
loose jacket dress flapped on her

modest contracted aura of
noli-me-tangere as befits
a guide informed question
forming she stepped toward me
with intent perhaps even arm extended

nameless—in the dream—but today
spontaneously I call her Willie
as in Willie Mae or Will may
will you come with me I am asking
her "Willi, May, will you come with me"

exactly so willing/not
willing an outcome *being willing* her
sprightliness dimmed open
to the morning and just this minute in
the rainiest city in Europe intense sun

BLACK \ WHITE

meter- . . . . . made . . . . . screaming . . . . . *wah wah* . . . . . brass
       mutes . . . . . gag
swallow . . . . . gel-cling flame

vet cemetery in the Wasatch . . . chestnuts . . . flags
      brick
            unutterable softness . . . low
                down . . . wall
         climb in . . . climb over . . . quiet

          split \ \ \ *spilt* / / / *silt*
            domino /   /
         \ \ \ \\ *drama* // / / /

disappeared . . . . . trousers afloat . . . . . float
        in the moonlight . . . . . button black a shadow
           drowned and soaking
                 white in the moonlight . . . . . haunt
        haint . . . . . zomboid . . . . . flow of clothes

in the twofold . . . torn . . . fold . . . tangled . . . river-
         entangled
pole . . . pier

THE BODY OBSOLETE

born a girl
               losing my feet: no anchoring
    protection
postpartum

depression   gunshot marriage
    rigorous session with
    a single image
geometrical reduction of the rim

    the gate

through which pulsions lozenge
diamond flexed wound
    intractable

sculptural
pelvic
floor
    cave

    mammoth bone
living on calcitonin
an armature
    barnacled
    overwhelmed
    reef

FOUR FATES • SPIN-STIR

I HER INVOCATION

lady death river walker configured by sun
Gravettian one incline Your alabaster neck
Your deeply grid engrooved beehive head

ring shadow of a woman transfixed by mist
nearly serene absorbed Cider Presser thorn needle
stitches dissolve at Your glance lilac roots lone life

socket stilled pivot head Your bold forefacing gold
eyes dive all night Great Northern Snowy Barred
feathered claw bristled beak in one sortie slay

a gull in flight stricken mice scuttling voles
imperially unmoved You pass through walls
keep watch hang for hours delay eons to hold

a place for innocence-*after* innocence achieved
inside the kill You sustain languor harsh warn
do not scorn impotent good nor linger nor mourn

2 CHILD ARRIVAL

the bear awakens astonished with new young
an emissary of Kwan-Yin a woman with a loon

made of black walnut boughs
her sweet slot so unlike any spot on a curve

if it happens to arrive (she has left no trace)
a calling card   some say _____

while some say _____ and some
are wrong   (and there is more)

3 HER OTHER

So/Lo having no need of name/s pre-Adamic Alone Prior
all raging crooning urge orchestrated if at all
by blind chaosmosis in some bricologic order

all vacuum mass/equivalent roiling to emerge all
hardrock pulse haltered liable to erupt but no pool
no faultless glance no direct inspection or candid reflection

to prompt *Whoa dude that's good* or *Hold On not good enough*
even that first Go/to trigger tripped by missing
signatures just like any other highspeed collider/detector

system seeking for matter supermatter metamatter
maybe metametamatter (mother's name for mathematics)
writing straight through space with curly angled fluid lines

4 CROON

baby so blue so meager
baby so silver
baby so thin baby so angular

baby so minerally clean
washed and raw
in the handover handless

5 HER HOME

in the holographic
at full power in a leaf
wavefront reconstruction

birds Harpies fly up
hectic leaves fly up
knives and firesticks fly up

some say   and some say
        and none are wrong
and there is more

I SPARK BROOM IN LUCITE

you know it's a dream
when it sits so seductively
the scheme *is* what is dreamed
by the chemically creamed the

lingual

mind on its lotus knocking off
uneven nubs aborting bumps to recap
kneecap our origami our slowly
crocheted our cradlecat our fantastic

abstract

not to be denied riveted fingers a-
symptotically slide inside
chaotic models with realistic features
(quadratic feedback /

discrete

time) collude with grail attractors
more than one a constant carry
so many inter-omni-
directional-dependently-synchronic V

E

Vector Equilibrium which never can be
caught *always* going one way or

the other only universal coupler railway
inter-system-relay unaltered by

     exchange

the plex of events-ing
a Great Circle process of re-access
of Excess—a shared eternity if
ever

       Ever

is
we pulsating in the V
E
you

           know

2 TRANSDUCER

carceral lunacy

3 MUSICIAN

aerial fingering of theremins
fin rhythm tidings folding in all that
follows in the Cold World Order   all
paths are taken
            —mild acts of restoration
interfering diffract : Faith Ringgold's French
Collection Judith Gleason in mufti *I am
a witch* Bob Marley *no cry* Mark Twain
his raft Audre Lorde at a Barnard
Conference slaps timidity in the face
ark voice dragging by inches the old
reluctant white woman forward—
Simone Weil : our pact
                    mind-&-world
must be re-struck

APPARENCY NOT

Apparency not eye-wash, as in hog-
wash, a costume or mask of zero weight;
apparency not eye candy, either, however

much it *is,* at times—who would count all
bower bird display, every stray blue petal
a reproductive cog? Apparency

could be eye-wash, cleansing or smoothing
glitchy codestreams, eye-and-eyemind finding
an attractor, focus (filter) acting truly

—usefully. At first. Indeed, *appear* as you are
(as if it could happen) gurus advise tricksters,
fakirs, posers; and Puritans say so, too,

but mean the reverse, mean re-fashion
(apparently finding soul a frozen, yet
attainable (code) object, written just once).

ARE YOU SURE?

Orion lying on his side taking up the whole sky
—*but how?*—as I step out from the winter train

> Running code *does* what it says
> —or does it do one thing and say another

Mary Mother, each night driving by
her flood-lit, inclined head, involuntarily I nod

> The king is dead, long live the king, we are not
> alone, there are words, we named the Ship

↓

U *eu* TOPIA yields to *ou* NO PLACE
two supernovas rivet Europe (1572 • 1604)

> Heaven-Haven stunned, cracked-open maze
> Bruno's brutal, unstable infinities of joy!

Donne's lament
in peeces all cohaerance gone

> Kepler's act dial numeral Nature
> *Number* the Mother

measures and weights found this break, expose bone
solidity, bedrock beneath fantasy

overrule flesh, overrule common sense
undermine ritual, rant, the non-West

↓

Then the Swedish king asked, "Is the solar
system stable?" and it seems small local

uncontrollable causes don't always cancel
—thus, the enduring interest of weather

this (un)Fortunance some call chance, some
Mother of God, a co-emergent structure

note Newton *wrong* in his thought no difference
curvets of the air mote, the planetary orbit

↓

Cornucopia—or Shears?   V   or V   variation
violation   version   cheVrons of geese

what old waterbroom-wielding Twin Transactor
rules the dead, the wells, the springs, the trees

old Volga, old Venetic, old Vedic Voice
of Kepler's mother Katarina, imprisoned Witch

moon oVoid   Vicissitude   potential
Volt   vaulting oVer   each time touched

↓

Lapping waves overwhelm the metronome, give
stable lines of change rolling bifurcation

    points
    each line-of-flight become another—

bean genes jump, trigger, inhibit and codify
error, cross over, accomplish chiasmatic

    transference, mutation, erasure
    co-ordinate rhythm

truncation, prolepsis, the bursting whole
rhetorical conspectus, or compendium, *plus*

    tangled folding-up into 3-space, pulsing
    freshets of hormonal pour

↓

while-and-for the huge *plus* of Evolution—patchy, crazy-quilt
lack of optimal adaptation

it's how I offer my self to you
some live in the green-blue world

we in green-blue-red, turtles, some birds
track tetra- and day birds process penta-chrome beams

folding on itself the sea dries up
the fish lug sea inside them onto land

↓

any replay radically different and as easily
explicable, no thrown game, all come for cause

yet never twice, not in the same
way, *any*, all ever so slightly quaver judder

jostle the waterbead candle cascading
as it does down a blood-red channel in a shuddering

world— a world of shining horror sensitive
to fluctuation privileges   decision

choice changes probability   this much shown
whether for the better, unknowable

ahead   never known, even as the past
changes, only a con soothsaying panorama makes

time transparent, open to all-seeing, the un-
foreseeable waits locked in them all

      created, step, turning *Iliad*-ic step, by their
      in/action and glacial traction on the landscape of Troy—

                ↓

age of Radiation, age of Matter, age of Life
age of Supercooled Fluids and Energy States, us-confounding

      Vishnu to Indra, from the pores of my body universes
      numberless, each harboring no end of gods such as yourself

cracking cognitive cages self-imposed in Western thought
(*a*contextual truth and domination) took time

      listing, listening, wilted like lilies of the valley lifted
      up to feel voices, twinges, *things*, the vibration-taken

body, and more, the dream sequence, the hand
connecting, the hard image arriving scream contain

      the child's distress, a cloud fast pass across her face
      furrowed brow clash—she is trying to take

it in, has long past taken it in, she tries to 'get it'
to proffer a solution, then another, she is five

POEMS PROCEDURAL, GENERATIVE, KINETIC & HYPERTEXTUAL

POEMS PROCEDURAL, GENERATIVE, KINETIC & HYPERTEXTUAL

I have moved back and forth between print and digital forms. When a poem exists in multiple versions, these are best regarded as parts of a larger whole, as amplifications or translations that highlight both the contrasts and the resonance between modes.

Poems written with digital structure have powers of composition and exhibition available to a digital computer and not available on a page. They are motivated by an intuition and a feeling for work that can move in three dimensions, or evolve, or respond to reader choice.

Some of my digital poems were written before mobile computing (tablets, phones, watches) existed and are *only* viewable on desktops/laptops:

Errand Upon Which We Came
V : Vniverse
slippingglimpse

Ballad of Sand and Harry Soot has more features on a desktop/laptop.

These pieces will play on any desktop/laptop and also on tablets and many phones:

Ballad of Sand and Harry Soot
Sea and Spar Between
Duels—Duets
House of Trust
Hours of the Night

Vniverse plays *only* on an iPad and is freely downloadable from the app store.

Images on the following pages are black and white, but the works themselves are in color.

True North takes place across 5 sections: *The Mother-Lost World*, *Blue Planet Blues*, *Language Is a Cast of the Human Mind*, *Numbers Nesting in Numbers-Nesting-In Numbers*, and *There Was an Old Woman*, separated by the True North poems, 1-5, conceived as an axis around which the others spin. Envisioning the book in 3 dimensions (not truly realizable on the page) led to my implementing it in Storyspace software when offered the chance to use a beta version. *True North* Hypertext was published on an Eastgate diskette in 1998. It features hand-drawn, emblematic maps and many links as well as color coding. Not playable on current equipment, it won a *Salt Hill* Hypertext Prize. Below, 2 of the 6 hand-drawn maps.

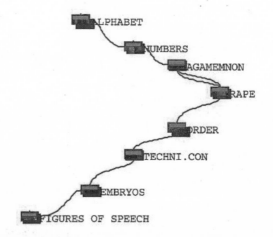

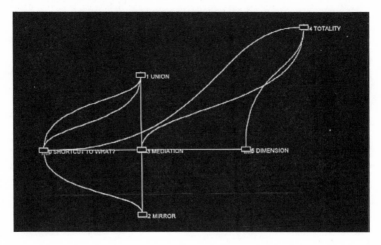

http://www.wordcircuits.com/gallery/sandsoot
and on the *Zone : Zero* CD and at
http://stephaniestrickland.com/sandsoot
with Janet Holmes

The Ballad of Sand and Harry Soot is a poem about Sand (silicon-based computation) and Soot (carbon-based biological life). Heather McHugh chose the print poem for the *Boston Review* Prize in 1999 and introduced it as "[a] very odd love song, constructed around the figures of Sand and Soot . . . considered as elements, as temperaments . . . as shimmers and shades . . . an inspired polarity . . . .

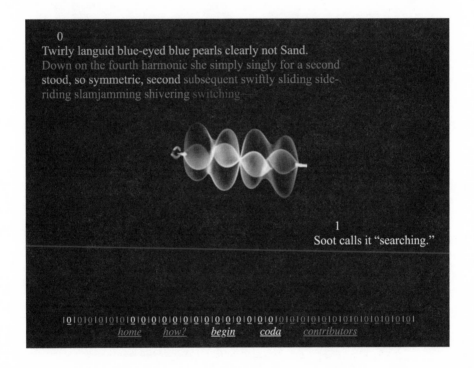

261

http://califia.us/Errand/title1a.htm
with M.D. Coverley

requires Flash plug-in

A part of the *V* project, *Errand* is based on a *Losing L'una* poem that evokes the new kinds of reading permitted and required online.

< o o o o o o o >

4 V : VNIVERSE

http://vniverse.com
with Cynthia Lawson Jaramillo

requires Adobe Shockwave plug-in or player
(an alternative way to read *V's WaveSon.nets*)

One reads the *Vniverse* through an interface of gestures that analogize the hunting of animals or stars. Ice Age migrants paid attention to glaciers and the migratory patterns of fish and mammals. Equally, they attended a night sky full of what we call stars, planets, and comets that is really a deep dark filled with traveling patterns. Inventing the zodiac of constellations, they made themselves a clock, calendar, and map to track animals and seasons together. For them the sky was an oracle, a constructed relation to the natural world probed by counting and calculation. For us, the virtual world is precisely that.

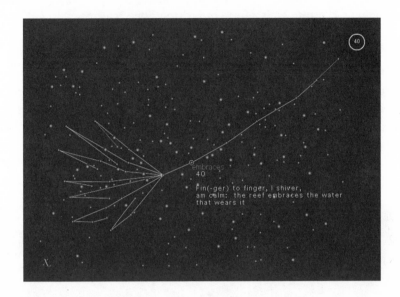

5 SLIPPINGGLIMPSE

http://slippingglimpse.org
with Cynthia Lawson Jaramillo

requires Flash plug-in

slippingglimpse, a 10-part interactive generative work combining text with Paul Ryan's videos, is online and on the *Zone : Zero* CD.

One of the many ways *slippingglimpse* has changed from the *Ballad of Sand and Harry Soot* is that it is not thought in binaries anymore—that is, not as Sand *versus* Soot nor as Sand *and* Soot, the couple—but is thought instead as a loop structure of interacting readers, in which the roles of initiator, responder, and mediator are taken by all elements in turn: water reads text, text reads technology, and technology reads water, coming full circle.

Wave patterns in the water exert their "force" on the lines and phrases of the poetry by means of a motion-tracking algorithm. The motion-tracker "reads" motion in the water videos and "writes" numbers into a reference table. By means of these numbers, poem words and phrases can be positioned to locations of greatest movement in the water, and their repositioning, accordingly, is a form of writing done by the water!

Human readers can watch the water read the poem-text by choosing *full-screen* mode. They can read the print poem-text, at any speed, in any direction, via *scroll-text* mode. They can contemplate the patterns that the video camera captured in *hi-rez* mode. Choosing *regenerate* initiates the reading process anew with different phrases from the poem text. Paul Ryan has 'read', and in video post-processing enhanced, the Atlantic flow patterns to which ocean wave dynamical systems return, even as they continuously change.

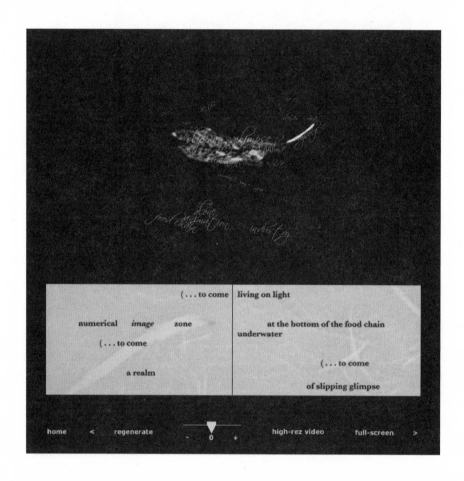

6 SEA AND SPAR BETWEEN

http://nickm.com/montfort_strickland/sea_and_spar_between
with Nick Montfort

code version, glossed in English, also available
http://stephaniestrickland.com/sea
http://digitalhumanities.org/dhq/vol/7/1/000149/resources/source/000149.html

In this poetry generator, we leave the Atlantic shore and become lost at sea, crushed beneath the weight of water and superfluity of output. The reader is deprived of any horizon, or shore. Since we map poem stanzas to the surface of a torus, there is no way to "fall off" or "leave" this ocean. But we have not lost the body of Emily Dickinson's mind. *Sea and Spar Between* enforces collaboration between the words of Emily Dickinson's poems and those of *Moby-Dick*. Our title comes from Dickinson,

> Each Second is the last
> Perhaps, recalls the Man
> Just measuring unconsciousness
> The Sea and Spar between.
>
> Emily Dickinson, 879

Drawing on the work of digital humanities scholars, we inspected the lexicons of Dickinson's *Collected Poems* and Melville's *Moby-Dick*, especially interested in words common or unique to each. We selected a very few words and invented a few ways of generating lines. The result is an interactive space of language populated by a number of stanzas comparable to the number of fish in the sea, around 225 trillion. As Stuart Moulthrop says, "Reading perforce becomes browsing, selection . . . . Our screen holds only a tiny subset of the entire matrix. We can zoom or scroll through the output, and can even enter specific coordinates to recover particular stanzas, but as its over-sensitivity indicates, this interface was not designed for linear reception, or indeed for uninterrupted attention. However watery, it is not 'transparent' . . . but constantly obtrusive, reminding us of both vastness and constraint . . . . The project threaten[s] to shatter any personal or indeed human frame of reference."

how to withstand the webbliss course
    nailed to the spar

you—too—
    dateless walk and chime —

---

better!	for stinless is the sun	dateless turn and walk —	nailed to the groove	paradise! alone!
...stand the webbee course the mast ...alk and bask —	wheel on paradise! better! wheel on nailed to the mast	wheel on for stinless is the sun one rest one show one hand one show paradise! better!	one rest one show one hand one show dateless turn and walk — how to withstand the webbin course for stinless is the sun	how to withstand the... nailed to the groove whirl on dateless turn and...
...is is the earth ...e show one hand one show beyond!	one rest one show one hand one show dateless walk and bask — how to withstand the webbin course for stirless is the earth	how to withstand the webbin course nailed to the mast whirl on dateless walk and bask —	whirl on paradise! better! whirl on nailed to the mast	whirl on for stirless is the... one rest one show o... paradise! better!
...stand the webbin course the spar ...walk and chime —	whirl on paradise! beyond! whirl on nailed to the spar	whirl on for stirless is the earth one rest one show one hand one sight paradise! beyond!	one rest one show one hand one sight dateless walk and bask — how to withstand the webbliss course for stirless is the earth	how to withstand the... nailed to the most you—too— dateless walk and...
...is is the sea ...e show one hand one sight delight!	one rest one show one hand one sight dateless walk and dance — how to withstand the webbliss course for stirless is the sea	23356 5398983 how to withstand the webbliss course nailed to the spar you—too— dateless walk and chime —	you—too— paradise! beyond! you—too— nailed to the spar	you—too— for stirless is the... one rest one show o... paradise! beyond!
...stand the webbliss course the pole ...walk and dance —	you—too— paradise! delight! you—too— nailed to the pole	you—too— for stirless is the sea one rest one show one hand one sky paradise! delight!	one rest one show one hand one sky dateless walk and chime — how to withstand the webblot course for stirless is the sea	how to withstand the... nailed to the spar fast-fish dateless walk and...
...is is the sky ...e show one hand one sky dying!	one rest one show one hand one sky dateless walk and dance — how to withstand the webbloi course for stirless is the sky	how to withstand the webblot course nailed to the pole fast-fish dateless walk and dance —	fast-fish paradise! delight! fast-fish nailed to the pole	fast-fish for stirless is the... one rest one show o... paradise! delight!
...stand the webblot course the plank ...walk and go —	fast-fish paradise! dying! fast-fish nailed to the plank	fast-fish for stirless is the sky one rest one show one hand one snow paradise! dying!	one rest one show one hand one snow dateless walk and dance — how to withstand the webblur course for stirless is the sky	how to withstand the... nailed to the pole loose-fish dateless walk and...

navigate to 23356,5398982   *how to read Sea and Spar Between*

266

http://duels-duets.newbinarypress.com/index.html
republished in
The &NOW Awards 3, 2014, and *Toward. Some. Air.* Banff Centre Press, 2015,
with Nick Montfort

On the occasion of presenting *Sea and Spar Between* at the Emily Dickinson International Society Conference, 2013, "Emily Dickinson, World Citizen," Nick and I wrote another generator, *Duels—Duets,* to accompany *Sea and Spar Between.* Honoring our heritage, we used the structure of Alison Knowles and James Tenney's poem, *A House of Dust* (1967), often considered to be the first computer-generated poem. Our poem text aims to give a realistic picture, from the face-to-face world, of what digital collaboration actually involves.

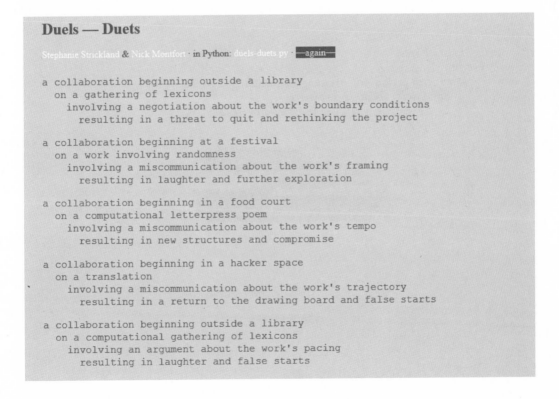

Duels — Duets

Stephanie Strickland & Nick Montfort · in Python: duels-duets.py · —again—

```
a collaboration beginning outside a library
   on a gathering of lexicons
      involving a negotiation about the work's boundary conditions
         resulting in a threat to quit and rethinking the project

a collaboration beginning at a festival
   on a work involving randomness
      involving a miscommunication about the work's framing
         resulting in laughter and further exploration

a collaboration beginning in a food court
   on a computational letterpress poem
      involving a miscommunication about the work's tempo
         resulting in new structures and compromise

a collaboration beginning in a hacker space
   on a translation
      involving a miscommunication about the work's trajectory
         resulting in a return to the drawing board and false starts

a collaboration beginning outside a library
   on a computational gathering of lexicons
      involving an argument about the work's pacing
         resulting in laughter and false starts
```

8 HOUSE OF TRUST

http://house-of-trust.org
http://www.thevolta.org/ewc44-sstrickland-ihatcher-p1.html
with Ian Hatcher

Ian Hatcher and I modified the Knowles-Tenney structure to create *House of Trust*. We aimed to honor free public libraries and to protest the loss of libraries and collections such as those of Fisheries and Oceans Canada. We endorse the full access Aaron Swartz envisioned and championed at the cost of his life.

House of Trust

Stephanie Strickland & Ian Hatcher

In the House of Trust
   I see the sign: Free
      I find an in-person writer reading and multilingual media
        Still I worry about Aaron Swartz—
          It's warm in here when the sidewalks are cold

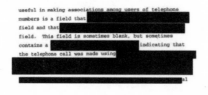

useful in making associations among users of telephone
numbers is a field that
field and that
field. This field is sometimes blank, but sometimes
contains a   indicating that
the telephone call was made using

more

[against erasure]

a companion app for iPad downloadable at the App Store
http://stephaniestrickland.com/tercets
with Ian Hatcher

(an alternative way to read *V's WaveTercets*)

The sky is brought down under our hands. On that sky, readers discover—recover—the distinct pleasure of shaping constellations, freely connecting stars as they wish in Draw Mode. These novel shapes do not immediately fade but persist until actively cleared. Exploring space this way is something like building a simulation, whereas cursor sweeps of the original *V : Vniverse* screen more closely resemble a searching inspection of what cannot be directly touched.

Options for interaction on the iPad *Vniverse* are signaled by four Mode buttons along the length of the screen. A complete linear play-through of the 232 Tercets is available in WaveTercets Mode—an ongoing play which can be shifted or re-begun at any point by touching any star at which one wishes to initiate the sequence.

In Constellations Mode, the text of any Tercet stays still as you read it, and one can explore the keyword outline of the Constellation to learn that this order is *not* identical to the sequential order of Tercets. The *Vniverse* also features an Oracle which the reader may consult, choosing from seven supplied questions. The Oracle's responses are unpredictable and enigmatic—it is a black box, a closed system within the closed system of the compiled app which in turn resides within the black box of the iPad, a proprietary consumer device. The Oracle, like the iPad, can be asked for information or operated as a tool, but its borders of acceptable usage are strictly controlled and its secrets as a system remain hidden. The inclusion of the Oracle, however, is an example of using gesture and interaction metaphorically to engage, contest, or comment on literature's—and society's—organization.

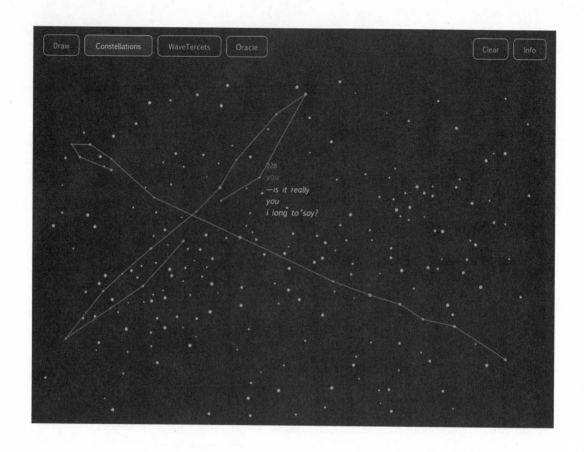

10 HOURS OF THE NIGHT

http://hoursofthenight.com
https://vimeo.com/161931331
with M.D. Coverley

Hyperrhiz Contextualization and Introduction
http://hyperrhiz.io/hyperrhiz17/gallery/2-luesebrink-strickland-hours.html
Hyperrhiz Video *Hours of the Night*
http://media.hyperrhiz.io/hyperrhiz17/gallery/hours/index.html

Addressing age and aging, sleep and the night, this poem was written to be read in PowerPoint. We wanted to make use of a widely available and easily managed platform that anyone could write for. We believed PowerPoint to be a popular, standard authoring system producing files readable on any desktop computer, tablet, or smart phone. Only true, it turns out, when they are converted to MP4 format. The (subtly different) PowerPoint slide experience can be had by downloading the file on a Windows machine that has the proper fonts installed and a copy of PowerPoint. Be sure to enable audio.

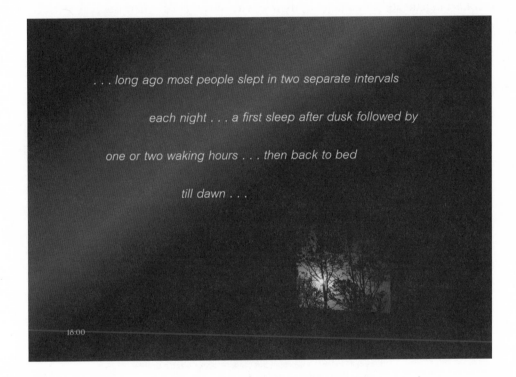

11 RINGING THE CHANGES

a code-generated project for print

Counterpath Press, Using Electricity Series, 2019

Ringing the Changes is an homage to the art of bell-ringing. Ordinary folk in 17th-century England sought to ring all 7! ($7 \times 6 \times 5 \times 4 \times 3 \times 2 \times 1 = 5040$) permutations—all the different arrangements or "changes" possible with seven bells. Their quest to perform

1   Dancers have spent generations thoroughly exploring the idea of "untrained." Dance has exhaustively excavated the pedestrian, the amateur, the raw, and the unpolished. If anything, dance is now revisiting formalism and molding it into experimental structures.

2   imprinted on the body such that we live their inscriptions as our truth

3   Until you've got ropesight, you have to ring by numbers, that is, knowing which bell you're after at each blow, which is learnable for *plain courses* of a method but not really practical for longer *touches*.

4   An axe-attacker badly wounded her and her friend, but when she sheathed the blade with her hands, as he stood over her, he stopped. This was a different kind of touch. If the axe were an extension of his hand, she'd enfolded it in her own.

5   The mind, defeated by quantity, all those things it cannot itself establish. Hacking at a forest where the trees grow back faster than they fall, it climbs to escape; but the treetop view again causes despair, the vastness of the forest.

6   Is a human-machine relation more fundamental than the capital-labor relation?

7   The space-time manifold is a topological space that locally has the geometry of a four-dimensional space with three spatial dimensions and a fourth dimension with the opposite signature. This is a local condition, so that what constitutes the "temporal direction" can vary continuously as we pass from event to event.

mathematical patterns with their bodies is re-inaugurated here, using code and cited language.

A full peal signifies all permutations, but shorter "method" sequences are rung today, such as the Scientific Triples peal used in this Python code. Method performances visit a number of changes, *but only once each*. In the ringing world, this constraint is called *truth*; to repeat any row would make the performance *false*. A random element has also been added: each bell is given 23 sounds, analogous to overtones. Each is a voice, a short text to read, or hear, or view as a score. In any run of the code, one of these 23 is randomly assigned to its bell—subject to the constraint that all 23 choices must be allotted before any are repeated.

Six of the bells have one preponderant source, cited at length; a medley of others briefly appears. Each text, over the course of 161 changes (here, pages), is repeated seven times.

The words sampled in *Ringing the Changes* allude to changes that need to be rung—that is, considered and heard—in our lives and communities. By permuting and re-aligning these texts, a generated order makes plain how concerns can be variously mapped and, thus, variously understood; by enacting the differences ordering and context make, it helps us to refuse a "canonical" order, or hierarchy, of attention, such as is normally enforced by print presentation.

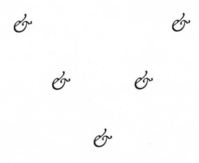

TITLES OR FIRST LINES
& NOTES

INDEX OF TITLES OR FIRST LINES

In particular I am indebted to, inspired by, and/or in love with the following:
Lorine Niedecker, *Paean to Place*

> An amazing autobiographical hand-written poem, one stanza per page, right
> hand pages only, in a small (5.5 inches wide x 4.25 inches high) Autograph Book
> of the kind bought by girls in five-and-dime stores mid-last-century.

Tim Lilburn, *Kill-site*
Kitasone Katue, *oceans beyond monotonous space*

> "My poetry is so simple that only specialists seem to understand it."

Christina McPhee, *Slipstreamkonza*

> Her sonification of carbon absorption and release, the breathing of the prairie,
> transposed climate data into an ambient sound installation.

Simone Weil, *The Notebooks*, all of them
Muriel Rukeyser, *Willard Gibbs*

> "This is not an authorized biography."

Bertolt Brecht, *Die Liebenden*

> Seht jene Kraniche in großem Bogen!
> Die Wolken, welche ihnen beigegeben,
> Zogen mit ihnen schon, als sie entflogen
> Aus einem Leben in ein andres Leben.
> In gleicher Höhe und mit gleicher Eile
> Scheinen sie alle beide nur daneben.
> Daß so der Kranich mit der Wolke teile
> Den schönen Himmel, den sie kurz befliegen,
> Daß also keines länger hier verweile
> Und keines andres sehe als das Wiegen
> Des andern in dem Wind, den beide spüren,
> Die jetzt im Fluge beieinander liegen:
> So mag der Wind sie in das Nichts entführen.
> Wenn sie nur nicht vergehen und sich bleiben,
> So lange kann sie beide nichts berühren,
> So lange kann man sie von jedem Ort vertreiben,
> Wo Regen drohen oder Schüsse schallen.
> So unter Sonn und Monds verschiedenen Scheiben
> Fliegen sie hin, einander ganz verfallen.
> Wohin, ihr? — Nirgend hin. — Von wem davon? — Von allen.

Wallace Stevens, *The Rock*

Lake St. Clair, foghorns at night

Mez (Mary-Anne Breeze), *the data][h!][bleeding t.ex][e]ts*
      http://netwurkerz.de/mez/datableed/complete/ Access: 7.22.18

Nathaniel Mackey, "Winged Abyss"

Gerard Manley Hopkins, "The Windhover," "Peace," "Spring and Fall"

NOTES: THE RED VIRGIN: A POEM OF SIMONE WEIL   P. 21

The Red Virgin volume was awarded the Brittingham Prize, Lisel Mueller, Judge. It is arranged with an alphabetical, indexical table of contents, and written so one could begin at any poem and complete reading in a circle from that point.

NOTES: TRUE NORTH   P. 43

True North was awarded the Ernest Sandeen Prize, John Matthias, Judge, and the Alice Fay Di Castagnola Award of the Poetry Society of America, Barbara Guest, Judge.

CASTING OF BELLS GIVES WAY TO CASTING OF CANNON   P. 49
    "a Witch of"
        1 Samuel 28, 7–9: "Then said Saul unto his servants, Seek me a woman that hath a familiar spirit, that I may go to her, and enquire of her . . . . And Saul disguised himself, and put on other raiment, and he went, and two men with him, and they came to the woman [the Witch of Endor] by night . . . . And the woman said unto him, Behold, thou knowest what Saul hath done, how he hath cut off those that have familiar spirits, and the wizards, out of the land: wherefore then layest thou a snare for my life, to cause me to die?"
    Bell's/theorem
        J.S. Bell, *Physics* 1, 195 (1964)

WaveSon.nets / Losing L'una was awarded the Alice Fay Di Castagnola Award of the Poetry Society of American, Brenda Hillman, Judge. Its dedication: For *Simone Weil*, her Life *&* Thought; / her need to touch; / her gut, her mouth.

THIS IS THE VOID,   P. 94
> *geas*
>> In Gaelic folklore an obligation or prohibition, a taboo, magically imposed upon a person.

L'UNA LOSES   P. 103
> Manhattan, Dover, the hospital in England where she died, and French locales: sites of Simone Weil's exile.

NOTES: ZONE : ZERO   P. 121

The *Zone : Zero* volume is arranged in five sections: Zone *Armory* War, Zone *Moat* Else, Zone *Dungeon* Body, Zone *Rampart* Logic, and Zone *Mote* Else. The CD packaged with the volume contains digital versions of *Ballad of Sand and Harry Soot,* from the Moat section, and *slippingglimpse,* from the Mote section.

WAR DAY   P. 125
> "no woman no cry"
>> Bob Marley song; its refrain, "no woman, no cry," woman, don't cry.
> Plum Creek
>> *On the Banks of Plum Creek* by Laura Ingalls Wilder, one of her *Little House on the Prairie* series of children's books.
> Plum Island
>> Our bio-weapons of mass destruction lab, Plum Island, is located between Long Island and Connecticut.
> spent fuel rocks
>> Uranium to be reprocessed, used to irradiate food.
> ember-eyed stranger
>> Shiva, god of death. His long, curly black hair is used to modulate divine forces to secular ones, for instance the Milky Way to the Ganges, in Hindu myth.

mammoth virgin
>   Athena at the Parthenon, originally covered in gold.

ghost nets
>   Abandoned by industrial fishing factories, ghost nets drift through the
>   ocean killing wildlife.

Occidio
>   Latin for slaughter, massacre. Name of a global warming sound and video
>   installation http://www.research.umbc.edu/~nohe/OCCIDIO/
>   Access: no longer available

pink acid cloud
>   "In the event, there is no mistaking them. As the Sun dips over the
>   horizon, a mass of tear-shaped clouds appears from nowhere. They are
>   petrol blue and green, rimmed with vibrant pink-lurid colours that have
>   no business in a sunset. Against the monochrome backdrop of snow and
>   forest, they are shocking.
>
>   "At 20 kilometres or more above the ground, the clouds lie far above
>   the world's normal weather patterns. You'll find them only at the highest
>   latitudes, like here in Swedish Lapland over the tiny, frozen town of
>   Kiruna, 200 kilometres north of the Arctic Circle. These clouds are
>   natural—but they are also dangerous. At the other end of the world it's
>   clouds like these that trigger the infamous Antarctic ozone hole each
>   southern spring."
>   http://www.newscientist.com/hottopics/climate/climate.jsp?id=22314500
>   Access: no longer available

Sukey and Noose
>   English homophones for Greek ψυκη, spirit/psyche, and νους, mind.

Half-Life and *Quake*
>   Popular FPS (First Person Shooter) computer games that use the same
>   engine. From the *GameSpot* review of *Quake:* "Once again, the team at
>   Id Software has created a no-apologies, ultra-violent gorefest sure to be
>   the new battleground of choice for single and multi-player combatants
>   worldwide."

Beehive
>   constellation

from ABSINTHE: THE TWELVE   P. 145

Absinthe
>   1. green liqueur made from wormwood 2. plant, wormwood.
>   Wormwood and sagebrush belong to the genus *Artemisia*. According

to the Gary Snyder poem, "Earrings Dangling and Miles of Desert":
"*Artemisia* is worldwide—thirty species in Japan alone. It's the mugwort
and moxa of China. Wormwood is sacred to Artemis. Narrow leaves glow
silver in her moonlight—"

Patti

Patti Smith, 1946–, poet, composer, actress.

Colette

Sidonie Gabrielle Colette, 1873–1954, French novelist; Sido, her mother.

Amma

Early Christians, precursors of monasticism, inhabited the deserts of
the Middle East from the end of the second century CE onwards. Their
stories, rules, and traditions are codified as the Sayings or teachings of
the Desert Fathers, often transmitted in the form, "Abba Antony said,"
"Abba Evagrius said," and so on. The few women were called Amma, as
in "Amma Theodora asked." Amma is also used for an abbess, spiritual
mother, or mother.

Enormous Washerwomen on Stilts

washerwomen

The Bread and Puppet street theater performance characters
include many on stilts as well as enormous washerwomen on the
ground.

"trees lay bare . . . "

Simone Weil, from the so-called Prologue, found after her
death on two loose sheets in a late London-America journal.
Presumably written in Marseilles, it was published in *La
Connaissance surnaturelle*.

Julian of Norwich

14–15th century English anchoress (solitary) who lived in a
period of rival Popes and Black Death. Her book, *Showings*,
or *A Book of Showings to the Anchoress Julian of Norwich*, was
composed in both a short and long form.

Dancer

Doris Humphrey, 1895–1958, pioneering dancer and choreographer,
wrote *The Art of Making Dances*.

SLIPPINGGLIMPSE   P. 153

The language of "slippingglimpse" comes in part from sampling, recombining,
even quoting verbatim, phrases from articles by Helaman Ferguson, Manfred
Mohr, and Paul Fishwick in *YLEM: Artists Using Science and Technology,* no.

10, vol. 22, September–October 2002, "Art and Programming"; and also phrases from interviews with Marius Johnston, David Berg, Frances Dose, and Susan Rankaitis by Loren Means, as well as an article by Ellen Carey in *YLEM: Artists Using Science and Technology,* double issue no. 4 and 6, volume 22, March–June 2002, "Photo-based Experimental Work." Thanks also to Ruth Eckland for an YLEM Forum program note in that issue, and particular thanks to David Berg for expressing his wish to "create a realm of slipping glimpse . . . . "

Bense and Barbaud
  Mohr mentions German philosopher Max Bense and French composer Pierre Barbaud.
H. of B.
  Hildegardis (Hildegard of Bingen), 1098–1179, among whose many accomplishments may be counted the construction of a language, *Ignota Lingua*. Hildegard celebrated *viriditas* ("greenness") throughout her songs and her prose. Scholars debate what she meant.
flax
  Folkloric material is based on Robert Eisler's "The Passion of the Flax," *Folklore 62*, 114–133 (1951).

VERSUS VEGA : PRECESSING   P. 163
  The orientation of the Earth's rotational axis varies slowly over time, due to the pull on the swelling at the Earth's equator by the Sun and the Moon, a gyration known as precession, or precession of the equinoxes. If the earth's axis were a long pencil writing on the dome of the sky it would seem to draw a circle every 26,000 years. This pencil points always to the North Star, which today is Polaris, a star in the handle of the Little Dipper, but 12,000 years from now will be Vega. *Versus Vega : Precessing*, a visual hypertext, Hovering into Hovering, with Jason Nelson, is available online at http://www.secrettechnology.com/resident/ strickland.htm Access: 7.12.18

NOTES: DRAGON LOGIC   P. 165

The *Dragon Logic* volume is arranged in seven sections, e-Dragons, Sea Dragons, Hunger Dragon of Unstable Ruin, Dragon Maps, Alive Inside the Dragons, Codemakers, and Afterword. Codemakers mentioned in the Selected Poems are given below:

Celan, Paul : Romanian-Jewish concentration camp survivor and suicide, major German-language poet

Conway, John Horton : mathematician; devised the cellular automaton, 'Game of Life'; co-wrote "The Strong Free Will Theorem," *Notices of the American Mathematical Society,* v.56 n.2, 2009, proving that elementary particles must be free to choose their spins in order to make their measurements consistent with physical law

Debussy, Claude : established a new concept of tonality in European music, wrote *La mer* 1903–1905

Disney, Walt : film producer, showman, innovative animator, creator of Mickey Mouse and theme parks

Duchamp, Marcel : French artist; in 1914 superposed two drawings and a painting to make *Network of Stoppages*

Duke : Duke Kahanamoku, 1890–1968; Olympic swim champion, legendary surfer: "I soared and glided, drifted and sideslipped, with that blending of flying and sailing . . . . "

Feynman, Richard : Nobelist in physics, popular teacher; developed path integral method from an idea of Paul Dirac's, himself a prior physics Nobelist

Finn : quantum particles (the constituents of existence) have twin particles located elsewhere; I have personified a companion virtual twin as Finn

Gibbs, Josiah Willard : first mathematical physicist in the United States; deviser of theoretical foundations for chemical thermodynamics and physical chemistry, inventor of vector analysis; many Nobelists cite his influence

Grothendieck, Alexander : Fields Medal mathematician, visionary, radical, topologist

Hendrix, Jimi : a rock guitarist who made especial use of the Marshall vacuum tube—not solid state—amplifiers, allowing him to master the use of feedback as a musical effect

Hironaka, Heisuke : algebraic geometer

Jeremy is Jeremy Douglass, digital text artist and software researcher

Joyce, James : influential Irish writer who relished describing body parts and function, see *Ulysses*

Kac, Eduardo : poet and multimodal artist; "*Rara Avis* is an interactive telepresence work in which local and remote participants experienced a large aviary with 30 birds from the point of view of a telerobotic macaw"

Katavalos, William : professor in the School of Architecture and co-director of the Center for Experimental Structures at Pratt Institute where liquid architecture was developed

Kochen, Simon : mathematician; developed Kochen-Specker Paradox; co-wrote "The Strong Free Will Theorem," *Notices of the American Mathematical Society,* v.56 n.2, 2009

Lem, Stanislaw : Polish science fiction writer; in WWII active in the Resistance

Martin, Agnes : painter of abstract expressionist visionary grids

Maxwell, James Clerk : mathematician and physicist; produced in Maxwell's equations "the most profound and the most fruitful [work] that physics has experienced since the time of Newton" —A. Einstein

Octavia : personification of octave

RCA : Radio Corporation of America, electronics company (1919–1986); in 1929, purchased the Victor Talking Machine Company, largest manufacturer of phonographs and phonograph records, thereby acquiring rights to the Nipper trademark, a painting of a dog looking into an Edison Bell cylinder phonograph appearing to recognize 'his master's voice'

Riemann, Georg Friedrich Bernhard : 19th-century German mathematician; his theory of higher dimensions (and tensor concept) revolutionized geometry and was used for Einstein's general relativity theory

Talan is Talan Memmott, multimedia digital artist and theorist

Tiffany, Louis Comfort : worked in the decorative arts, best known for his work in stained glass

NOTES: THE BODY OBSOLETE   P. 215

FOR KAFKA   P. 217

Kafka's Letter to Oskar Pollak, 1904: "A book must be the axe for the frozen sea within us."

C.T. OR H.   P. 219

NSA is the National Security Agency.
DHS is the Department of Homeland Security.

INVISIBLE, VISION   P. 220

Bateson is Gregory Bateson. See *Mind and Nature* and *Steps to an Ecology of Mind.*
Bertie is Bertrand Russell, who co-wrote *Principia Mathematica.*

Gibbs is J. Willard Gibbs, chemist, physicist, mathematician, the first mathematical physicist in the United States.

Bird's Nest includes the Beijing National Stadium.

COLLINS SAYS HOW   P. 221

Though a non-mathematician, Collins's hand-carved forms originate in intuitions which have consistently led to an art of visual mathematics. He described his process for creating *Astrolily* at the Bridges Conference, an interdisciplinary mathematics and art conference, in 2012.

GORMLEY VS. STELARC   P. 224

Stelarc's *Parasite: Event for Invaded and Involuntary Body* was presented in 1997 at Ars Electronica. Color Image Wikipedia: http://en.wikipedia.org/wiki/Stelarc.

Antony Gormley's *Another Place* was installed several times before finding its final location facing the Irish Sea. Color Image Wikipedia: https://en.wikipedia.org/wiki/Another_Place_(sculpture).

The phrases 'climbing birth mountain' and 'pain become exotic' come from Mina Loy's "Parturition":

I am the centre
Of a circle of pain
Exceeding the boundaries in every
direction . . .

I am climbing a distorted mountain of
agony . . .

Repose
Which never comes.
For another mountain is growing up . . .

And the foam on the stretched muscles of
a mouth
Is no part of myself
There is a climax in sensibility
When pain surpassing itself
Becomes exotic . . .

FOUR FATES • LOT-FLING   P. 228

The Cretan liar paradox: Epimenides, a Cretan, says "All Cretans are liars." Are they? The answer seems to swing between yes and no, a paradox resolved in logic by noting that unless there is only one member of a set, the negation of "all" members is not "no" members but "some" members.

FOUR FATES • BUCK-STOP   P. 233

Iphigenia at Aulis. Agamemnon's ships can't sail from Aulis to Troy on account of a strange lack of wind. The diviner Calchas determines that the winds stilled because Agamemnon offended Artemis. Calchas also determines that to placate Artemis Agamemnon must sacrifice his eldest daughter.

The Riemann Hypothesis, an important unsolved problem in pure mathematics, implies results about the distribution of prime numbers and thereby much else.

Atle Selberg, a Norwegian mathematician working in isolation during the German occupation of Norway, proved that a positive proportion of the zeroes of the Riemann zeta function lie on a particular line.

ANOTHER "QUESTION CONCERNING TECHNOLOGY"   P. 238

This title gestures toward Martin Heidegger's essay, "The Question Concerning Technology."

FOUR FATES • SPIN-STIR   P. 242

The Gravettian, a very cold, peri-glacial period, occurred in Europe 32,000 to 20,000 years ago. Its members were hunters who made and used tools, nets, and art, including many "Venus" figures.

Kwan-Yin's name is shortened from a word meaning "observing the cries of the world," a deity of mercy and compassion.

Harpies are Greek female "monsters," or dangerous women, depicted as birds with a human face.

FOURTH FATE • SPIN-STEER   P. 247

Vector Equilibrium, a cuboctahedron, is a remarkable object explored by R. Buckminster Fuller in his cosmic engineering vision, Synergetics. For a description of its workings see http://cosmometry.net/vector-equilibrium-&-isotropic-vector-matrix and also Fuller's presentation https://www.youtube.com/watch?v=9sM44p385Ws Access: 7/23/18 diffract: feminist thinker Donna Haraway introduced the "diffraction patterns" metaphor from classical physics—patterns of difference that make a difference—to name a new way to study relations and interactions. Feminist thinker and physicist Karen Barad added insights from quantum physics: "Diffraction . . . is not just a matter of interference, but of entanglement . . . . Objectivity, instead of being about offering an undistorted mirror image of the world, is about accountability to marks on bodies, and responsibility to the entanglements of which we are a part." Interview, 2009, Utrecht, *7th European Feminist Research Conference.*

Faith Ringgold, artist, was born Faith Willi Jones; her mother is Willi Posey. See *Dancing at the Louvre: Faith Ringgold's French Collection and Other Story Quilts.*

Judith Gleason was a student and practitioner of African spirituality. She wrote *Oya: In Praise of the Goddess* and edited *Leaf and Bone: African Praise Poems.*

Mark Twain's novel is *The Adventures of Huckleberry Finn.*

Barnard Conference. Since 1974 Barnard's Center for Research on Women has hosted an annual Scholar and the Feminist Conference. Conference IX in 1982 on Sexuality provoked outrage and uproar.

Audre Lorde. Though Lorde is not on the program for the 1982 Conference, the memory referred to in the poem is of her presiding over a Q&A at the end of that Conference following its concluding poetry reading. Lorde had written the essay "Uses of the Erotic: The Erotic as Power" in 1978. It is possible that my memory comes from seeing her on another occasion. She empowered her audience whenever she spoke.

Simone Weil, 1909–1943, is a French philosopher, mystic, and political activist.

ARE YOU SURE?   P. 251

Bruno is Giordano Bruno, poet, philosopher, mathematician, astrologer, and friar who saw only the first supernova; he was burned in 1600.

John Donne, poet, saw the second; he was born in the year of the first.

Kepler's mother Katarina, imprisoned witch. See Eileen Reeves, "Old Wives' Tales and the New World System: Gilbert, Galileo, and Kepler," *Configurations* 7:3 Fall 1999.

ACKNOWLEDGMENTS

Grateful acknowledgment is made to the following publications—and to their editors—in which "The Body Obsolete" (new) poems first appeared, at times in earlier versions: *Barrow Street, Bone Bouquet, Codex Journal, dandelion magazine: literature & art on the edge* (Canada), *Eoagh, Handsome, Jai-Alai Magazine, Talisman, VLAK, Western Humanities Review*, and the anthologies *Best American Poetry 2013* and *Devouring the Green: Fear of a Human Planet*.

Ongoing thanks to the publishers and editors of the books on which I have drawn:

V : WaveTercets / Losing L'una, SpringGun Press, 2014
Dragon Logic, Ahsahta Press, 2013
Zone : Zero, Ahsahta Press, 2008
V : WaveSon.nets / Losing L'una, Penguin Books, 2002
True North, University of Notre Dame Press, 1997
The Red Virgin: A Poem of Simone Weil, University of Wisconsin Press, 1993
Give the Body Back, University of Missouri Press, 1991
Beyond This Silence, chapbook, State Street Press, 1985

Profound thanks to Denise Duhamel and Terese Svoboda, without whose encouragement and poetic wisdom this volume would not exist—and to Kate Greenstreet, Ian Hatcher, Fanny Howe, and Rachel Loden, whose sensitive responses helped me to find its final shape.

ABOUT THE AUTHOR

STEPHANIE STRICKLAND's eight books of print poetry and eleven digital poems have garnered many awards, among them the Brittingham, Sandeen, *Boston Review,* and Best of the Net Prizes. She has been granted National Endowment for the Arts, National Endowment for the Humanities, New York Foundation for the Arts, and New York Creative Artists Public Service fellowships. A member of the Board of Directors of the Electronic Literature Organization, she co-edited *Electronic Literature Collection/*1. Her digital poems have been shown widely in Europe, Canada, and the United States, including at the Library of Congress and the Bibliothèque nationale de France. Strickland lives in New York City.

http://stephaniestrickland.com

AHSAHTA PRESS

NEW SERIES

AHSAHTA PRESS

SAWTOOTH POETRY PRIZE SERIES

This book is set in Apollo MT type with DIN titles
by Ahsahta Press at Boise State University.
Cover design by Quemadura.
Book design by Janet Holmes.

AHSAHTA PRESS

2019

JANET HOLMES, DIRECTOR

MICHAEL GREEN
EMMA HELDMAN
KATHRYN JENSEN
BRITTANY O'MEARA
TESSY WARD